Bear ~~instrument~~ in All Seasons.

A
CHOSEN
SEED:

from Mustard Seed to Abundance

Blessing and Love

DENISE S. BENNETT

D S B H

919. 612. 7078

All scripture, unless otherwise noted, is taken from the New King James Version. Copyright © 1982 by Thomas Nelson, Inc. Used by permission. All rights reserved.

ISBN: 1453804153
ISBN-13: 9781453804155
Library of Congress Control Number: 2010913364

Dedication

• • •

In life's busyness and the hustle and bustle of each day, we often forget to slow down, count our blessings, and appreciate the richness of our heritage and legacy. Our family has been honored with a jewel full of wisdom that's sometimes undervalued. **A Chosen Seed** *is dedicated to my entire family with the desire that we take the fruit from this SEED to grow and nurture our personal, business, and spiritual lives.*

To my husband, Ricky Bennett Sr. for your marvelous rainbow filled with love and support over the years and especially throughout my injury and this project. Through all of the pain, your graciousness, crazy sense of humor, and unwavering spirit kept me sane with a focused purpose. You carried me from the moment of a broken ankle to this glorious moment of completion. Your love is immeasurable.

Like a proud peacock flashing with colorful feathers, to Dion, Ricky Jr., and Clayton Bennett: thank you for being strong, big thinkers and aspiring young men full of favor. God has a mighty work for each of you. This book will be a guiding seed light for Deanna Kaylene, Donovan William, and all of the other Bennett grandchildren to come.

And of course, to Granny, who is the inspiration behind the book. And for my parents, Carnell Troy and Bennie Ledrew Shird: I am **A Chosen Seed** *because of you.*

Acknowledgements

This compilation was a labor of love. For all of the family members who assisted in recanting this wisdom, thank you.

*To Joanne Drane and Nell Hinton for your unselfish acts, expertise, diligent work ethic, and contributions to making **A Chosen Seed** a best seller: thank you.*

Since this book was completely written while I was out of commission with a broken ankle and blood clots, my sincere love and gratitude goes to all of our friends and family who prayed for us, loved us, visited us, and fed us, physically and spiritually. While you were praying, God was performing miracles and providing total restoration. I will always have fond memories and especially for my birthday party on the couch with my foot properly positioned high up in the air. What a sight! Though I was in intense pain, it was a most high and extraordinary gesture. To Tina Berryman, Earline Middleton, Janet Puryear, Janis Quarles, Barbara Simon, and Lorraine Stephens: you are the greatest.

Marsha Kay Sherrod, for your unselfish giving, thank you. To Michelle Rich Goode who encouraged me to read The Path, *for it crystallized my purposed VISION for this season.*

To the medical team of Dr. Constance Battle, Dr. David Fajgenbaum, Dr. Benu Chattergee, Dr. Wayne Smith, Dr. Elizabeth Campbell: thank you for allowing God to use your gifts, medical expertise, and talents.

Table of Contents

INTRODUCTION:

Inspired by a Century

———————— • • • ————————

Our family was blessed extraordinarily this year with our mother, affectionately known as "Granny," celebrating one hundred years of life. A century of life! Have you ever contemplated what life was like one hundred years ago? Some of us can't even imagine what life would have been like a few decades ago, so of the idea of a century is quite unimaginable.

My son, Ricky, in his research for Granny's centennial celebration, reminded us that one hundred years ago:

- Sugar cost $.04 per pound

- Eggs cost $.14 per dozen

- The average wage was $.22 per hour

- The average worker made between $200 and $400 per year

- The average life expectancy was forty-seven years

- 95 percent of all births took place at home

- Only 14 percent of all homes had a bathtub

- Two out of every ten adults couldn't read or write

- Only 6 percent of all Americans graduated from high school

- There were only about 230 reported murders in the entire USA

- Maximum speed limit in most cities was 10 mph

- The highest structure in the world was the Eiffel Tower

Amazing, isn't it? Even more amazing is that someone has survived and thrived for a century. Spearheaded by my cousins Sabrina McCoy and LaShaunda Steele, Granny was honored at a beautiful celebration, a grand affair planned and executed by her grandchildren and great-grandchildren. Traveling from all over the country, relatives and friends attended that we hadn't seen for many years. I was awestruck that this was a glorious occasion and not a gathering due to a tragedy or funeral, the normal instance when several hundred people gather.

Sitting at the Lakeside Event Center in Whiteville, NC, I wondered why Granny was chosen to live for a hundred years. Why were we, the members of her family, chosen to be a part of this particular family and from this particular seed? While the mystery remains, it is an incredible dream that many families could only wishfully desire, increasing the appreciation of the blessing.

A seed, according to Dictionary.com and Wikipedia.org, is:

- A ripened plant ovule containing an embryo

- ❧ A source or beginning

- ❧ Offspring

- ❧ Family stock; ancestry

The purpose of all seeds is reproduction. They come in all different sizes, shapes, and colors. The outer covering of a seed is called the seed coat. Seed coats help protect the embryo from injury and also from drying out. Seeds remain dormant or inactive until conditions are right for germination. All seeds need water, oxygen, and the proper temperature in order to germinate. Some seeds require proper or specific lighting to mature. The quality of the end result often depends on a combination of the quality of the seed combined with the right conditions in order to yield an abundant crop.

This is what is so fascinating about Granny's centennial celebration: the kernel of one seed that Wiley Royal and Ada Anna Shaw planted a century ago has culminated into an offspring of nine children, forty-four grandchildren, thirty-six great-grandchildren, and six great-great-grandchildren. Two of her children, Lonnie Troy and Carl Troy, are now deceased.

The parable of the mustard seed found in Luke 13:19 is an extraordinary parallel to our family. The mustard seed was often planted by farmers in Palestine. Matthew and Mark point to the seeds' small size and contrast these with the size of a full-grown tree. Beginning as an embryo, the size of a tiny mustard seed, Granny's offspring have developed, matured, and blossomed into ripened abundance. This life-fulfilling abundance esteems our family stock with five living generations, assuring bountiful growth for generations to come. What started in Whiteville, NC as a mere mustard seed has produced full-grown fruitful trees chosen to grow all over the world. So why are we a chosen people? After being awakened from a dream, I was led to Deuteronomy 7:6, 13-14:

"God has chosen you to be a people for HIMSELF, a special treasure above all the peoples on the face of the earth. 13: And HE will also bless the fruit of your womb and the fruit of your land, your grain, and your new wine and your oil, the increase of your cattle and the offspring of your flock, in the land of which HE swore to your fathers to give you. 14: You shall be blessed above all peoples."

Like a mustard seed, none of us can determine our family genealogy, where we are kernelled, or when life begins. There's an old saying that applies here: "you can choose your friends but not your family." We have to make the best of everything that's given to us. While our family was not born into wealth, the intangibles are filled with riches and abundance.

One of the enhancements that our family and many others have received is the ancestry wisdom poured into us. As Granny and my deceased grandfather, Arnie Madison Troy, Sr., raised me, there are many old wise sayings of which, as I grew older and when life's challenges and circumstances knocked me over, the true meaning became apparent.

Like scriptures, these wise sayings, or *Grannyisms*™ are seeds that provide peace, comfort, protection, instruction, and navigation. *Grannyisms*™ may have a variety of interpretations depending on the circumstance or situation. Ringing in the back of my head, they have been life-saving for me, as a catalyst for making sound business decisions in the corporate and entrepreneurial arena, raising three wonderful and aspiring young men, dealing with employees and colleagues, pioneering in the commercial lending environment when neither women nor minorities were supposed to be viable candidates, and being the light at the end of the tunnel in racial and gender intense moments. These *Grannyisms*™ gave me permission to exceed others' expectations and to not apologize for my passion for excellence even when unexpected. This passion for excellence transcended into raising the bar for our sons, my banking colleagues, employees, friends, community involvement, volunteering, and everything of value in my life.

Like *Grannyisms*™, sayings of the wise are to be heard and heeded, particularly in this season of harsh economic and financial times. As a society, with unprecedented advances in education and technology, our increased knowledge and advancements have resulted in a loss of wisdom along the journey. The harsh reality of the recession has caused us to venture back to the basics, giving a higher credence to these wise instructions. Their deep meaning has a unique way of reprioritizing one's thoughts, engaging in what is really important: love, family, friends, and health. Amazingly, the older people in our lives never told us how to solve a problem but would always give us a *Grannyism*™ with deep implications; some to be felt as a sharp, potent bolt of lightning many years later.

Many of these *Grannyisms*™ are well-known sayings, deriving mostly from unoriginal expressions passed down for generations, pulpit reflections, messages from songs that brought comfort during depressed and enslaved conditions, scriptures, and the plain ups and downs of life. Still others are self-taught, lessons learned from past experiences and mistakes. No matter the origin, they are full of laughter, light bulb moments, and strategic navigation for centuries to come. Even with the broken English, the meanings bring hope for *A Chosen Seed* to reach its full potential and bear great fruit. Like a mustard seed, they begin as a tiny thought in passing. After marinating in your heart and spirit and then applying them to your everyday personal and business life, over time their powerful meanings lead to abundant and "back to basic" living.

If we capitalize on lessons learned and unselfishly share the wisdom to others, we all have the potential to be a CHOSEN seed and a CHOSEN people. If you have a strong foundation, like a mustard seed, once you're planted, nourished with water for survival, nurtured with compassionate care, pruned because of necessity with oxygen and proper lighting, your personal and professional life will be filled with beauty and abundance.

Every single one of us remembers a *Grannyism*™ shared with us at some time in our life. If it wasn't imparted by a family member, every CHOSEN seed can reflect on a wise saying that remains pressed as an indelible mark in our hearts. Whether it was intended to encourage, instruct, motivate, or guide, this wisdom coming from hard knocks and common sense can rescue our country if we would just slow down and allow it to order our steps.

This book is intended to provide answers to allow one to navigate through life with discernment, seeing beyond the surface of life's problems and solving the intimate puzzles that keep you up at night. It has profound implications for business owners and leaders, sales associates, religious leaders, parents raising children, couples weaving their lives together as one, women everywhere who are juggling a dozen balls, trying to keep them all in the air, and individuals, young and old, who share a passion for excellence. I have found myself over the years using some of these *Grannyisms*™ in professional speaking engagements, business strategy, and financial sessions to further explain a financial or life principle. Business professionals find them fascinating as they make the perfect analogy more vivid. These *Grannyisms*™ are excellent coaching, teaching, mentoring, and parenting tools. They provide leadership instructions with applicable light bulb moments. When illuminated, they provide a crystallized vision to excel. These chosen seeds of wisdom will lead your business, personal, and spiritual life from a mustard seed to abundance.

You are *A CHOSEN SEED* and this is your season to come out of the land of lack, transformed from a tiny little mustard seed to a life filled with growth, maturity, richness, and abundance.

CHAPTER 1

Soil Preparation

• • •

Farming was the main source of daily preservation and revenue in Columbus County, Whiteville, NC where we grew up. Before sowing any type of seeds, it was crucial to till the soil and properly prepare the soil to ensure that a great crop would flourish.

Like life, tilling is a timing process. Precise timing can be everything and make all the difference in the world for a bountiful crop. Farmers took great pride in their crops and, to ensure that the soil was in the best condition, they added nutrients to the ground by fertilizing. Fertilization enables the seedbeds to be of their utmost quality in order for the chosen seeds to produce incredible results.

These mustard seed wisdom strategies found in this collection will add foundational fuel for you, your business culture, and your spiritual strength.

Foundation

• • • •

> ৵ **When you have faith of a mustard seed, you can do anything but fail.**

A mustard seed is extremely tiny, about one millimeter in diameter; it is larger than many plants, such as poppy, columbine, peppercorn, and dandelion. Once planted, it grows into a huge tree. Since failure was not an option, it was Granny's faith, as well as the faith of others born in that era, that championed them through trials and tribulations, hoping and praying that tomorrow would be a brighter day. With little or no monetary means, faith is all that they had.

So what is faith? Faith is certainty, dependability, and builds confidence! Whether we choose to acknowledge it personally or corporately, faith permeates every day of our lives. Faith gives us strength during difficult and tumultuous times. It is our sustainer; it is even strong enough to move mountains. It was Granny's continuous and constant faith— the size of a mere grain, a miniature mustard seed—that was big enough to pull her up by her bootstraps to a better life. That faith has resulted in unthinkable opportunities, which will sustain her legacy for future generations. She truly believed that with this miniature sized faith, one can do anything but fail.

Hebrews 11:1 and James 1:6 respectively provide quintessence: "Faith is the substance of things hoped for and the

2

evidence of things unseen." "Having no faith and doubting is like a wave of the sea, driven and tossed by the wind."

A beautiful song rendition titled "His Will" by William Steward III affirms: "When you have faith the size of a mustard seed, you can do anything but fail. Just put your trust in the Master's hand. Follow his will and obey his command."

❧ Make sure you have a strong foundation.

A foundation is support and the fundamental principle for everything that happens in life. From Granny's perspective, a strong foundation was education. Having only graduated from the eighth grade, she knew for her nine children that education meant a better life and a priceless ticket out of poverty. In his centennial reflection, my son Dion reminded us that she would always say, "Chillen', whatever you do, get in them books and get your education." This demand is now evident as six of her nine children are college graduates. Dion reflected that her grandchildren and great-grandchildren continue this legacy, being represented as preachers, educators, teachers, technical directors for major news organizations, postal executives, sales executives, engineers, mechanics, business and financial analysts, fraud/money laundering investigators, computer programmers, insurance administrators, bankers, business owners, chefs, key office personnel, and many others. If you have a strong foundation with education, you can weather many storms.

❧ **Hard work will take you to a land flowing with milk and honey.**

Hard work was a non-negotiable, an avenue to sweeter days stimulated by the nourishment that only milk provides and as sweet as honey. We envision the Promised Land, flowing with milk and honey as rich, fertile, bountiful and trouble free. In Exodus 3:7-8, Moses was at the burning bush and the Lord said: "I have surely seen the oppression of MY people who are in Egypt, and have heard their cry because of their taskmaster, for I know their sorrows. So I have come down to deliver them out of the hand of the Egyptians, and to bring them up from that land to a good and large land, to a land flowing with milk and honey."

This *Grannyism*™ is a vital lesson on success: a work ethic that prepares one for life's multiple challenges. The persistence of hard work eventually provides one with a lifestyle compared to being in a luxurious land flowing with milk and honey. In business, your work ethic will distinguish you from your competition, setting you apart with distinction and excellence. Even Hebrews 12:11 tells us that hard work, discipline, and chastening bring joy, yielding great fruit from your seeds. "Now no chastening seems to be joyful for the present but painful, nevertheless, afterward it yields the peaceable fruit of righteousness to those who have been trained by it."

❧ **Life is simpler when you plow around the stumps.**

When it was time to get the seed beds ready for a crop, Daddy used the mule to plow the dirt in preparation. Since our heat came from the woodstove, there was always a stump in the yard, forcing you to maneuver around it when playing and doing outside chores. They were all around, in the front yard and backyard, even near the edges of the road. This lesson paints the stumps as the trials that come from daily living. Before you can plow around the stumps in your life, you first must know where they are located. Life is simpler when you ignore the things that don't matter, whether they are in front, beside you, behind you, or across the road. Plowing around the stumps simplifies things; you will experience an innate amount of trouble (stumps) merely because you are blessed enough to be alive. So plow around some of your troubles and leave them in the dirt.

ᛉ **The early bird gets the worm.**

Getting up early and preparing were the sure signs that you were going to have a great day. Granny encouraged—or shall I say required—everyone in the house to get up, get dressed, and prepare for the day by the time the sun came up. During tobacco season, when the rooster crowed—and believe me it was early, usually anywhere between 5:00 and 6:00 am—that was your cue to get up, and at least pretend that you were awake. People that arose early were considered successful. Most people who lived on a farm accomplished more by 10:00 am than most people today accomplish in the entire day.

In the business world, the early bird is the employee who gets to work early, is fully prepared, and has a well-thought-out strategy for the day. The worm is the reward from this executed plan.

❧ **If you believe your vaccine will work, then inject it in your own veins.**

Injecting a vaccine in your veins ensures its immediate circulation. This is a powerful leadership principle. When you are preaching, teaching, and coaching others, if you think the advice or instruction that you are giving has value, then you should be using it yourself. In other words, live what you preach. If you do not show the advice that you're giving to your family, friends, or colleagues in your life, injected in your own veins, then you have not properly tested the vaccine.

❧ **A slack hand makes you poor.**

Growing up, we were always busy. There was no time to sit and relax. No one could have a slothful spirit and survive. This actually derives from Proverbs 10:4-5, which says, "He who has a slack hand becomes poor. But the hand of the diligent makes rich. He who gathers in summer is a wise son; he who sleeps in harvest is a son who causes shame."

On the farm, during gardening season and particularly during the summer, crops were plentiful. We canned vegetables and put up food in the freezer in order to have it in the winter. We made serious preparation to have adequate meals during the months when food wasn't plentiful.

As you think of your personal and business life today, remember that preparing for unexpected times is a key to a stress-free life. In business, what are you doing when your competitors are sleeping? What strategies are being implemented to turn a transaction into a relationship?

ɤ   Live your life so folks can trust you.

To people in Granny's generation, trust was everything. When people trusted you, it elevated your integrity because this meant that you held in confidence one's most intimate and vulnerable circumstances. With trust comes faith and predictability in creating an environment where others are comfortable to excel. Trust in business positively affects profitability. There are studies that show customers who trust you not only purchase more but revenue can be increased by as much as 80 percent. Looks like Granny should have been in some corporate boardrooms.

ɤ   Everything that glitters ain't gold.

When something sparkles with brilliance, it is often superficial with flashiness. When things in life appear to be grand, with lots of sparkle and luster, at the end of the day the true facts often reveal the glitter. In astonishment, the glitter quickly turns into a tarnished fixture.

In business and spiritual settings, an enduring and constant elegance is simply a camouflage of the truth. Over time, experience and discernment will allow you to determine the motives of others, pure or impure. This, especially, is a lesson of which our young people should be cognizant. Deceptive ways that appear to be beautiful on the outside may merely be fake glitter.

ɤ   Your word is your bond.

A bond is intended never to be broken. When you give someone your word that you'll do something, then you should do everything possible to get it done. Your word, in Granny's time, was considered all that you had; an honor, a reputation to uphold.

If your company develops a mission or vision statement, is your word your bond? Are your mission and vision statements merely eloquent words or is there a daily sacrifice to live up to them?

❧ **Winners do what losers don't want to.**

A thin line exists between winners and losers. Winners don't whine and complain. They take what life dishes out and turn it around for their good. No matter your profession or stage in life, this is applicable to everyone and should be incorporated in one's personal and business strategy. This piece of wisdom should be taught to children at an early age. The sooner this is digested, the more quickly a fuller and more complete life can be crafted.

❧ **You will reap what you sow.**

Quality seeds produce quality results. Consequently, an ill-prepared crop bed and seeds deficient in nutrients produce like results. In order to reap quality results, you must sow quality seeds. In these unprecedented economic and financial times, we deserve the results we are getting. Greed in the industry is the end result of the havoc reaped. Particularly in the lending industry, many programs brought about multiple opportunities to make money, from 100-percent financing to option adjustable rate mortgages with potential increases in one's house payments multiple times per year. It's a hard pill to swallow. All of us will eventually reap what we sow individually, corporately, and as a nation. "For whatever a man sows that and that only is what he will reap." (Galatians 6:7b, Amplified Bible)

☙   What goes around comes around.

Whatever you do, good or bad, it will be returned to you. The twin to reaping what you sow, this is a reminder that you can't outrun your deeds. No matter your speed, they will catch up with you. It seems that the bad ones move more rapidly than the good ones sometimes.

There were many reminders of the Golden Rule. What goes around comes around is an assurance that your bad habits and deeds will eventually catch up with you. If you do wrong, eventually you will be wronged, often by the same person or group that you offended or caused the injustice. If you have a history of having bad personal habits or business practices, your history will become the present.

☙   You can't make a horse out of a mule.

Mules were used to disk and plow the fields and were the subject of the most difficult work performed in the fields. Generally mules were stronger than horses, required less food, and were more highly intelligent. Horses were used to pull carriages and buggies, as they had more speed and a strong sense of balance. Their use in sports and recreation brought joy and revenue to their owners.

No matter how hard you try otherwise, you have to have the right characteristics to do whatever job you're assigned. Everyone has different gifts and talents, which should be developed to the fullest. While individuals may have many similarities, this wise saying lets us know that a horse and a mule are cut out of two different molds. On a sales team, there are horses and mules similar in experience levels, age, appearance, dress, and business protocol, but their performance measures will highlight the differences.

❧ **Be careful what you hitch your wagon up to.**

To hitch is to connect for the sole purpose of transporting. Wagons were hitched up to a horse or mule to carry supplies, vegetables, people, or other valuables. While it may appear to be easy, hitching requires skill, making sure all of the iron pins used to connect are perfectly aligned.

Hitching your wagon in life has dual implications. Be careful when you align yourself with different people, colleagues, and associates, because once you are aligned, their reputation, whether good or bad, is connected to you. Decisions about to whom you hitch up with may have lifelong consequences.

Aligning yourself properly can position you for future success. An improper alignment, just like with a wagon, can cause a trajectory collision. All of the valuables you are transporting in your wagon of life may be damaged or lost, costing you revenue, time, and energy. In some cases, the loss may be so devastating that no amount of money can measure the full value.

Make sure that the transporter to whom you hitch your wagon is strong enough to carry the load and have the proper tools for alignment to cement your connection.

- **Before you try to pull someone out of the water, make sure your feet are on solid ground.**

This is truly a lesson on financial management. Coming to the aid of family and friends is a wonderful gesture but make sure you have the stability to weather the storm yourself. We all need to be helpful or have a benevolent attitude, but when you find yourself pulling the same person out of the water all the time; you have become an enabler. Financing the bad decisions of others is not wise, especially when you're trying to maintain solid ground.

- **When life gives you lemons, make lemonade.**

Life is full of hurts and disappointments. This lesson on adaptability proves that while we can't control situations from happening, we do have the power to control our actions in responding. Making the best out of a bad situation is challenging but rewarding.

- **You never get a second chance to make a first impression.**

When making a first impression, you always put your best foot forward. The older generations were very strict when it came to discipline, manners, and cleanliness. You were told to be on your best behavior in all of your first experiences, whether it was meeting someone, a job interview, or even performing chores. Chopping weeds out of the garden had to be done to perfection, leaving not a twig in sight. The manner in which you performed was an impressionable tool resulting from how much pride, character and care were exhibited in your work. A great first impression was the distinguishing factor in putting you ahead of the rest.

⚡ You can't live but one day at a time.

All of us are guilty of worrying about tomorrow before it gets here. If we could learn to cherish each day, our lives would be filled with complete joy. In our busy lives, we can fall prey to overstressing about tomorrow such that we forget to enjoy today. Whatever you are being faced with, live only for today because tomorrow is not promised. One day at a time is all that we can handle. While it seems to be such a simple task, it's much more difficult to execute.

⚡ A small hole can sink a large ship.

These small holes were referred to as gossip, strife, a contentious spirit, laziness, a hardened heart, prejudice, and racism. Anything that you allow to fester in denial has the opportunity to bring to ruin to what could have been something of value. No matter how large your family, corporate enterprise, or religious structure, if you do not plug these holes very tightly, they will begin to sink your ship, as if you were in quicksand.

⚡ Hatred is like acid.

Acid is strong enough to corrode metal. Hatred, a very strong emotion, can also spread like wildfire, corroding and souring relationships. This unhealthy emotion can erode all of the good intentions of any entity, burning down to the foundational core.

ℸ **You can't get freshwater and saltwater from the same hole.**

This is a powerful foundational lesson on being authentic, true to yourself, having a strong value system, and being who you profess to be. This is not only a challenge to individuals but to every business that wants to thrive after surviving the current economic and financial crisis. The businesses that survive will indeed thrive. One who claims to deliver great service but never executes has neither fresh nor salt water running through their stream, just a tasteless liquid.

When I was a little girl, Daddy and his friend, Mr. Will Drayton, would go fishing and talk about what kind of fish were running depending on the month it was and whether it was a freshwater or saltwater fish hole. Being young and a fish lover, the meaning never registered with me; I just wanted the fish. However, his words resonated, especially when they would chuckle and Granny would give an example of someone living a saltwater lifestyle but on Sunday professing to be from the freshwater. Delicious fish come from both waters but you can't catch the same one from the same hole. Daddy and Mr. Will would bring brim, black bass, and mullets from the saltwater hole; catfish, perch, and trout came from freshwater. I thought that this was just talk, but it is biblical: James 3:10-12, "Out of the same mouth proceed blessing and cursing. Does a spring send forth fresh water and bitter from the same opening? Can a fig tree bear olives or a grapevine bear figs? Thus no spring yields both salt water and fresh."

Wow! Before you begin executing any plan, know what kind of results you intend to produce. Results from a freshwater hole may be entirely different than those from a saltwater hole. While the sales from the freshwater hole are profitable, saltwater strategies may cost you more money than the relationship is worth. *A Chosen Seed* can discern the difference.

۲ **If you don't have a seat at the table, you'll be part of the menu.**

Having a seat at the table ensures that you get to place your own order from the menu to your own specifications. This message has multiple meanings: to show up; be heard even if you have to speak in silence; and be a part of the solution and not the problem. When you sit around and complain, instead of creating your own roadmap, you allow yourself or your business to always be under attack.

The power of change rests in your own hands. Many think that others take away their power, not realizing that they are giving it to them. If you feel that you are a part of the menu, then take back your power and be accounted for. If you're out of sight, you're out of people's minds, having been placed on the menu as a temporary and seasonal dish.

۲ **We are the source of our own problems.**

Consider the problems that you or your businesses are currently facing. Now trace those back to the starting point of your initial decision-making process. It could be a quick hiring decision because you wanted to fill the position instead of applying some strategic planning measures. It could be bad financial positioning because you wanted something that you knew you couldn't afford. Whatever the case, if you allow honesty to penetrate: YOU are the source of your own problems in life as hasty decisions usually wreak havoc. Ultimately, only you can begin the correction and turn-around process.

꙳ A man's venom poisons himself more than others.

Poisonous venom is most commonly known in snakes or spiders. Here, it is analogous of the hatred or racism that someone harbors in their heart: it always comes back to bite them. A person's venom spewed through hatred, evil, wrongdoing, and deceit has a tendency to harbor inside the person, changing their whole demeanor. They never realize that their poison harms and damages their organs first before they infiltrate someone else.

When Daddy was bitten by a rattlesnake, it poisoned his entire system and plagued him with gout and pain for many years to follow. With proper medical attention, some of his pain could have been avoided. If bitten by a snake, knowing the kind is crucial to your vaccine and medical treatment. Recognizing and being aware of your venom can eliminate the poison from your system sooner.

꙳ You don't know what's in my alabaster box.

In Biblical times, alabaster was very expensive and the alabaster box was used only for the most important things, the finest of all finest. Alabaster was a symbol of purity and great honor. Past experiences, the precious minerals that have shaped your life in order for you to serve others are reflective of what is contained in your alabaster box.

The treasures gathered along the way and the endurance gained from one's tedious journey are the reason you and your business prevail even in tough times. Be appreciative of those struggles and experiences that have molded and shaped you. As represented in Matthew 26 and Luke 7, the struggles turn into strides and the experiences will result in higher elevations.

❧ **Rash words thrust like a sword.**

According to Wikipedia.org, a sword is a long-edged piece of metal, used as a cutting and/or thrusting weapon in many civilizations throughout the world. Rash words pierce just like a sword and the lingering damages are sometimes felt for years, even decades. We all are guilty of speaking before we think; particularly for persons in leadership roles, if you stick someone with a sword, you can pull it out. However, the thrust piercing from harsh words can never be pulled out.

❧ **If the cake is bad, you don't need the frosting.**

Growing up, we always prepared Sunday dinner on Saturday, including a delicious dessert. The significance of the frosting was icing on the cake, an enhancement to perfect ingredients turned delectable. Most of the times, the cake was so good, you didn't need any frosting; it was simply an added decoration.

In life and business, if your foundation is shaky, if preparation is lacking, if people don't trust you, if you have a contrite spirit or selfish intentions, then no amount of frosting can sweeten you up. In time, people will see through your motives and discover the real you.

❦   **Keep oil in your lamp.**

Anytime it was thundering and lightning, Granny made us turn all of the lights off, sit down, and be quiet. She told us that "the Lord is doing his work." Oil lamps were a staple, the sole source of light during a thunderstorm or when the electricity was out. Having a beautiful lamp without oil is useless so we were always prepared, sometimes only using the lamp oil a few times per year. Hearing this as a young child and young adult, I was clueless to the intended meaning. Having been in Sunday School every Sunday, I knew it had a biblical context. The parable is found in Matthew 25, where ten maidens had lamps; five of them were foolish and five of them were wise. The message of strength here is to always be prepared because you never know what tomorrow may bring. Oil is synonymous with truth and light. The lamp is a symbol of your life and its purpose. Keeping oil in your lamp is a warning against ill preparation. Adequate strategic planning has significant influence for business leaders as well. Don't wait until trouble parks in your driveway before you prepare for the unexpected. Keeping oil in your lamp brings security in the time of need.

❦   **Waste not, Want not.**

The best example of this is the current economic and financial crisis. When times are plentiful and money is flowing, we as a nation tend to spend, spend, and spend. In plentiful times, we should preserve in order to have adequate means to take care of us in the time of void, lack, and need. Our actions resulted in a liquidity crisis that caused the collapse of major banks and financial institutions, government bailout, and unprecedented foreclosures. The consequences of a wasteful attitude will result in a long-lasting avalanche for decades to come.

❧   **We make our habits, and then our habits break us.**

Habits are constant behaviors or patterns that we do without thinking about them. Since habits can have both positive and negative attributes, we have to be very careful to create habits that lead us in a positive direction. If negative habits are unchanged, they can break or destroy us. I am amazed at the significance and similarities of this piece of wisdom, as it compares to Dr. Stephen Covey's book titled *The 7 Habits of Highly Effective People*:

1.   Be Proactive
2.   Begin with the End in Mind
3.   Put First Things First
4.   Think Win-Win
5.   Seek first to Understand, then to be Understood
6.   Synergize
7.   Sharpening the Saw

Our habits can definitely make us or break us.

❧   **There's no testimony without a test.**

The root of a testimony is a test. You have to walk through the doors of pain in order to minister to someone else through their pain. When you have passed certain tests in life, people will cross your path and, during a particular season, you'll be able to provide them wisdom to put them on a safe harbor.

In business, once you've survived the political acid poured along the corridors; you are now equipped to keep someone else from getting burned. The test comes when you allow yourself to unselfishly pass this on to others.

❧ **Don't let Him catch you with your work undone.**

Now we've already established that growing up on the farm, you started the day early in the morning, usually at the crack of dawn. This lesson has spiritual connotations: when Jesus comes back, don't let Him catch you with your work undone. You have to be ready. As a child, I didn't believe this. From a child's perspective, I thought they told us this in order for us to work from sunup until sundown. Each of my siblings can recant personal testimony to "Don't let Granny catch you with your work undone." Personally and corporately, do the things that you intend to do today, because you have no idea what tomorrow holds.

❧ **A penny saved is a penny earned.**
❧ **Every penny has a purpose.**

The Great Depression began with the stock market crash in October 1929, when Granny was nineteen years old, her second year of marriage. Money was precious and powerful, and every penny was considered to be of great value. The average wage in 1910, the year Granny was born, was $.22 per hour. Picking up a lost penny from the ground and saving it was wisdom.

Everything in our household was made by hand. We made our own clothes, food, medicine and articles to use around the house such as brooms, baskets and soap. My sister,

Ruby Sterlyn Jackson remembers Granny impressing upon her that "since you can't make money, if you find a penny, pick it up and save it." Like a penny, very few things were discarded. Old items were transformed with quality into a secondary use while materials and scraps from dresses too small were converted into a signature trademark like a quilt or bedspread - priceless heirloom masterpieces.

A penny to Granny was likened to a trophy. Even today, using her walking cane as her assistant, she still picks up pennies. It certainly would have been less painful as a nation to have learned this exemplar lesson from Granny as The Great Recession is teaching us, every penny does have a purpose.

৵ If you never save any money, you'll never have any.

My brother Bill remembers our Granddaddy Wiley, Granny's father, instilling this into him as a youngster. Wiley Shaw, a free man, was born November 16, 1882, when I'm told his average income was approximately $20 per month. For Granddaddy, saving money was the norm for he knew what it felt like to be broke. Picking up a penny around his house was like a treasure hunt; we treated a penny as if it were a dollar. This is quite a valuable lesson in thrift for someone who owned his home debt-free and several acres of land when he died.

৵ Always save for a rainy day.

This is a contrast to Waste not, Want not. A rainy day is a parallel for a time of need and lack. It was instilled in all of us to always put something aside so you'll have resources in the time of need. Rainy days will shower both our personal and business lives. We must implement business strategies and establish a vision for the future. Wise decisions and smart allocation of spending will determine if it's just a shower or a rainstorm.

⚡ **An idle mind is a devil's workshop.**

The devil would take control of your mind if it were not stimulated. We were especially told this as young children: if you had too much time on your hands, with no goal or productivity in mind, you'd get in trouble. Honestly, I think this was another attempt to keep us busy. But as I reflect, I realize we didn't get into much trouble because we were too tired at the end of the day. An idle mind is also a lesson on slothfulness, laziness, and sloppy workmanship. A strong work ethic was developed at a very early age.

If your business practices are idle and you allow greed and complacency to infiltrate, your competition will devour you with takeovers and ingenuity. They will even utilize your own workshop space to excel.

⚡ **Parents who want to train their children in the way they should go, must first go in the way they want their children to go.**

Simply put, your example is much more meaningful and important to a young person in your family or people in the workplace than your words. You can influence those in your circle by how you live, not what you verbalize. You should never ask someone or expect something of your relationships, employees, sales team, or children that you wouldn't do yourself.

❧ **It doesn't matter what's on the table but what's sitting in the chairs.**

Tables are symbolic of a joyous occasion: enjoying great food with family and friends—our most valued assets. In Granny's era, older women showed their LOVE with a deliciously prepared meal. This was the glue that held things together, representing quality and a reward of love for the people sitting in the chairs. While the food was nourishing our bodies, it didn't matter if it was just beans and cornbread—it was very special for the people for whom it was prepared.

Corporately, if you have huge profits on the table and don't take care of your most prized asset—your people—then the profits are diminished. Value just as much what is sitting in the chairs as the well-prepared table.

❧ **Every tub has to stand on its own bottom.**

A tub standing on its own bottom is accountable, responsible, carrying and pulling its own weight. A tub that can stand on its own bottom shares a significant contribution and is accountable for its actions. Particularly as a member of a family or sales team, standing on your own bottom will maintain ultimate strength goals. A strong work ethic produces a strong bottom.

❧ **Every chair has to stand on its own legs.**

Every chair has four legs, sturdy enough to hold up an unbelievable amount of weight. This lesson is also about accountability and ownership. A chair has limited value or use in most cases even if there are three supportive legs.

22

As a team member, learn the skills to develop unshakeable leg strength.

☙ A chain is only as strong as its weakest link.

A weak link causes a chain to break. On the farm, everyone had chores. When everyone finished their respective duties, then everyone could stop and call it a day. A team is only as strong as its weakest link. As a team player, you never want to be the weakest link, as you will not only hinder progress but diminish core strength.

☙ You are always on stage.

This is the example you display to everyone with whom you come in contact. You never know who is watching you and whose life your stage presence is impacting. First impressions are lasting and the foundation for everything that came afterward. Your stage presence allows you to travel many places. With increased technology, including Facebook, Twitter, and many others, you are always on stage. Our performances should always reflect pinnacle success.

☙ A house divided can't stand.

A house divided refers to any unit sharing a common bond, such as a family, church, organization, or business. When that unit divides, it separates. When the unit is of one accord, it builds strength, accomplishing more as a team than individually. President Abraham Lincoln used a similar verse in a speech in 1858 regarding ending slavery, the source of which came from the Bible, in Mark 3:25: "And if a House be divided against itself, that House cannot stand". (KJV)

The implication is that united families, businesses, and religious organizations have insurmountable strength to sustain a foundation.

✷ Be wary of fair-weather friends.

Fair-weather friends are friends and colleagues in your personal and business life that are present only when things are going great. In good times, especially when you're on the top, you are surrounded by lots of friends, business, and church associates. In bad times or in times of need, you can't find them. On March 20, 2010, on my birthday, I broke my ankle riding a bicycle and ended up having surgery that added a permanent steel plate and seven pins in my right foot. Later a blood clot developed giving us a life-threatening scare. If you ever want to experience unconditional love, true friendship, and true relationships, then get sick, experience a life-threatening event, or stay confined for nine months. Fair-weather relationships go by the wayside, but true ones last forever.

Older people also caution to watch how friends treat you when you have money. Usually there are plenty of them. When the money gets funny and evaporates, so do your fair-weather friends.

✷ Don't waste your time learning the tricks of the trade; learn the trade.

This lesson breeds excellence from a quality education. A trade was considered to be a way to step out of an impoverished life. The command was not only to learn the trade but to be the best at it. By today's standards, we may have been poor in terms of dollars and cents; however, the lessons instilled were full of wealth, hope, dollars, and sense.

❧ The one who wins is the one who thinks he can.

If you think you can win at something, there's a high probability that you will. Your mind is your most powerful asset or your biggest deterrent. Winning in life is not always measured by money. Positively affecting the quality of life of others and then passing it on is much more rewarding. Winners know that they are winners simply by the power of their mind.

❧ Don't get too big for your britches.

Your britches are easily torn or ripped when playing outside. Getting too big for your britches meant that you were growing up too fast and wanting to experience too much of life, too soon. Getting too big for your britches was followed with, "You have all your life to be grown." In other words, enjoy the simple life of your youth that you have today. Tomorrow will have its own set of problems.

For the younger generation who is anxious to grow up too fast, this is one powerful piece of advice. You have all of your life to be an adult, full of responsibility and paying your own bills. Enjoy your youth while you can. Life passes by oh so fast!

❧ Stay in your lane.

This means to act your age and to take care of your own household or business instead of trying to meddle and take care of others' affairs. Handling your own affairs will keep you too tired to meddle in someone else's.

❧ **If you sweep around your own front door; you won't have time to sweep around mine.**

Sweeping around your own front door meant to take care of the business within your own household and not meddle in the affairs of others. Granny used to make brooms out of the straw from the fields. Sweeping was something you did even if the front porch didn't need it. This lesson means if you can take care of all that life throws on your plate, then you won't have any time to meddle in the affairs of others. Your broom is only strong enough to sweep around your own front door and does not have the capacity to sweep around the doors of others. We'd all prosper if we concentrated on the change we need to make in ourselves rather than the faults of others. There is a beautiful explanation written in a song by the Williams Brothers:

> "You know there are too many people trying to take care of other people's business and they can't even take care of their own. What you need to do is take six months to mind your own business and six months to leave other folks business alone. Sweep around your own front door before you try to sweep around mine."

❧ **I'm not driving that bus.**

My sister, Sandra Terrell, a retired educator, says this all the time. Driving a school bus was fun. During our high school years, school bus drivers were high school students. Only the most responsible, trustworthy students were chosen for this great task. We didn't realize at the time that this was a huge responsibility for sixteen, seventeen, and eighteen year olds. Like most others, I accepted the challenge just to have some income during the school year. While it was fun, it required skill, tolerance, discipline, patience, and attentiveness. This *Grannyism*™ meant that when something is none of your business and the solution rests entirely on the responsibility, skill, and control of someone else, there's no need for you to get involved. You can only drive the wheels that you control, which do not include your neighbors, your business associates, or any of your congregants. Steering your own life and driving your own bus is a full-time job.

❧   **There's more than one way to skin a cat.**

This has absolutely nothing to do with a cat, or any other animal. This means that there are many ways to accomplish the same goal or to do something. Brainstorming sessions are superb ways to tap the ideas of your entire team. The key is to be open to suggestions and give credence to all ideas. I've witnessed several corporate situations where one person will give their perspective and it's diminished faster than someone can turn off the light switch. Ten minutes later, the same idea is placed on the table by someone considered, shall we say, "the golden employee," and it's perceived as the best strategy since sliced bread. Be careful not to destroy the benefits just because of the benefactor. You can skin a cat multiple ways by embracing all of the creative ideas of other team members.

❧   **Be careful what you ask for; you just might get it.**

When we ask for something, we don't know the danger that it might bring nor do we take the time to consider any dangers. This was especially a directive when young people had new opportunities and wanted yet more, not realizing that some of the desires and wishes would be the cause of their demise. On the business front, the strategies being developed may be great ones but may detract from your core revenue stream. Adding one client but losing two is a high price to pay.

⚄ Don't bite off more than you can chew.

When you bite into a piece of fruit, you usually bite just enough to chew and enjoy each morsel. This compelling lesson regards the increase of material possessions, get-rich-quick schemes and anything that sounds too good to be true. This is a parallel to "live beneath your means," particularly as it related to acquiring the biggest house or vehicle that you think you can afford. It is far better to pace yourself for life's unexpected moments. When you have newfound money, an unexpected check, a windfall, or a new job with an increase or a promotion, it is wisdom and maturity that force you to pace yourself and not spend money just because you have it. Maturity develops when you have money and have no desire to spend it quickly.

This is so powerful and befitting today as we witness the financial stresses around the world. No one is immune to biting off more than they can chew, from the White House and government structure, to the sole proprietorship running a one-man/woman show!

There are many biblical warnings, such as Habakkuk 2:6-7: "Woe to him who increases, and to him who loads himself with many pledges. Will not your creditors rise up suddenly?

Will they not awaken who oppress you? And you will become their booty." When my sister, Sandra Terrell, reminded me of this *Grannyism*™, I was just taken aback at how this is earmarked and appropriate for the State of today's Union.

⚡ **You can't have your cake and eat it too.**

All celebrations are highlighted with a cake, scrumptious and with the potential to be sliced many different ways. Life is full of decisions, some having lifelong consequences. When faced with decisions to make, you can't have it both ways. You have to make a decision based on the facts you have at that time. The easiest path is not always the right path. The biggest slice of cake is not always in one's best interest. You may be biting off more than you can chew.

⚡ **What's good for the goose is good for the gander.**

A goose is a female, while the gander is a male. In today's context, if it's good for one person, it should be good for everyone. There shouldn't be a set of standards for one set of employees and another set for the others—usually at a lower status. I remember hearing this during the time that women were entering the workforce and the pay scales of male and female employees were imbalanced. It can also refer to rewards and punishment in any given situation.

⚡ **Do it right the first time. It'll take you twice as long to do it over.**

When Granny gave any of us instructions to do something, it infuriated her if we rushed through it and didn't follow orders. When we did it over, she would add something else to it, delaying going outside or whatever you were going to do. This is a great carryover into business. When you take the time to do it right the first time, you get closer to the finish line sooner.

⚡ **Build your hopes on things eternal.**

Hoping is the anticipation of something grand. Building your hopes on things eternal means to make sure you build your foundation on the things that really matter, eternal life, and not people and material possessions here on earth. It is better said in an old Negro spiritual, "Hold to God's Unchanging Hand":

> Time is filled with swift transition
> Naught on earth unmoved can stand
> Build your hopes on things eternal
> Hold to God's unchanging hand!
> Trust in Him who will not leave you,
> Whatsoever years may bring,
> If by earthly friends forsaken,
> Still more closely to Him cling!

⚡ **Ninety-nine and a half won't do.**

A foundation has to provide support for today and for future maintenance. This wise saying that Granny instilled provides a legacy in how you live and conduct business. Ninety-nine and a half won't do is the trademark or stamp that you placed on everything you did. Only 100 percent was considered a fulfillment of the job assigned, whether it was raking the yard, making your bed, cooking, or doing chores for the animals. Even when feeding the chickens or hogs, there was a spirit of excellence that came with the territory. It was unacceptable to do something merely well; only your best would do. What a befitting message to provide an incredible foundation to everything that we touch in all aspects of our lives. As *Chosen Seeds*, we'll bear great fruit.

Ninety nine and a half won't do!

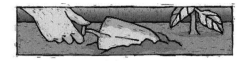

CHAPTER 2

Planting Seeds

• • • •

There's an art to planting seeds that is almost magical. Sowing seeds of greatness is congruent to the process of planting seeds. Before putting the chosen seeds in the ground, some seeds require a special treatment and some actually need to be soaked in order to reach their potential. Improper planting can be destructive and no amount of fertilizer, mulch, water, or special dirt will replace this importance.

Such is life. Let's compare planting with VISION. Everything begins with a VISION. It has to be defined clearly with strategies for execution to follow. These strategies and visionary execution have to be properly orchestrated for the phases of planting to achieve long-term success. The following *Grannyisms*™ provide such passionate orchestration.

The Vision

• • • •

ᴕ   **Ain't no harvest without seed time.**

Seedtime and harvest time each have their own order and value. You certainly can't expect to have a great harvest without the preparation and sowing of quality seeds. Harvesting is hard work but is absolutely gratifying once the grain or fruit is produced. This *Grannyism*™ teaches us the value of order and the need to take advantage of every second, minute, and hour given to us each day. This relates to our relationships in that nothing happens by accident. We can't rearrange the order of seed and harvest time, no matter how many shortcuts we take. Without a careful executed vision and planting of seeds, there will be no great harvest.

ᴕ   **Seeds bear fruit.**

Seeds, in this instance, are synonymous with people, particularly each of us as individuals. As *A Chosen Seed*, your life and everything you touch should produce fruit or something of value. Fruit is symbolic of excellence in our personal, business, and spiritual life. Business seeds bear great fruit, fueling our communities and economy with long-lasting succession.

ᴕ   **Bloom where you are planted.**

Bloom provides beauty and effervescence. Each of our lives has different seasons: infancy, youth, our educational years at all levels, marriage, children, careers, community service, and retirement, all represent seasons in which we are planted for a specific span of time. Find happiness and joy in every season in which you are planted. If you rush without fully blooming, you end up denying yourself of the culmination of the effervescent process of development. Live for today and enjoy the ride. Blooming where we are planted brings effervescence and a legacy.

❧ **Decisions have lifelong consequences.**

Many, if not all of us, have made decisions for which we have paid for decades, if not a lifetime. I knew what this meant as a child, but full comprehension came as I aged and matured. Depending on the circumstance, the cost associated with consequences from our decisions is exorbitant and pricey. The decisions we make not only affect us today, but tomorrow and in the years to come.

❧ **If you're not careful, you might end up in the hole you're digging for somebody else.**

The Shaw family has a family gravesite where all of our ancestors and loved ones are buried. During bereavement time, the funeral home will come and dig a hole for the grave, usually six feet deep. Digging a hole for someone else means that you have deceptive motives or are knowingly attempting to do harm. This was strict caution that you may end up in the same hole intended for someone else or the subject and victim of your own actions. When someone observed evidence of this happening, we would cite the Golden Rule. Matthew 7:12 (paraphrased): "Do unto others as you would have them do unto you."

❧ **Common sense ain't common to everybody.**

This one is priceless. Something that appears to be standard operating procedure to one person can be extraordinarily difficult for another to grasp. The more educated as a nation we become, the more greed overrides common sense, getting us into trouble. The financial crisis comes to mind when I think of common sense: when investors created unlimited opportunities for mortgage qualifications, common sense should have screamed that the house of cards would tumble. It amazes me that leaders at the top chose not to see the tumbling until the whole house fell.

As business leaders, we should always seek best practices from the everyday people in our trenches. Common sense has a way of dwelling in the trenches.

❧ **In our good days, our weaknesses are revealed. In our bad days, our strengths are revealed.**

Our weaknesses are revealed when things are going well. When times are great, we seem to make careless decisions, not always considering what tomorrow might bring, showing the true essence of our beings. Greed, frivolous spending, quick decision-making, and poor planning often occur. In our bad days, we pray and draw upon our faith and strength. When times are tight, children are disobedient, your body is sick; you lose your job or a loved one: all these bring about strength that we never thought that we had. During these times, we are quick to pray and the potency of our true essence exudes.

♥ **Don't burn any bridges. You just might have to cross back over them.**

A bridge is a structure built to provide a passage, providing an avenue to cross from one place to another. It's a connecting point. The advice of not burning bridges is a beautiful mirror for life's transitions. Not being able to cross back over means that you've made decisions that can't be changed in the future, putting a permanent end to something. With unemployment at its peak, be careful how you leave your existing place of employment. After the anger subsides, you may have to go crawling back. Speak kind words of previous employers, team members, and seasonal friends. With mergers, consolidations, and acquisitions at their peak, you may need the help of some of your previous associates to provide a passage back across the river. You may have to ask permission of still others to cross back because they may end up being your supervisor.

♥ **Actions speak louder than words.**

Words without actions are mere consonants and vowels. The words, "I love you" are spoken so frivolously these days that they sometimes loses their effectiveness. Growing up, we rarely heard these words verbally, but love was just inherent because of how family treated us and provided for us. The older generation believed that it was better to SHOW that you loved someone than say it. Their actions spoke volumes and it really never had to be said.

♥ **Talk is cheap.**

When a person continuously talks about all of the things that they are going to do but never executes them, this is talk being cheap. Anyone can brag, boast, or give false hope but it takes a disciplined and special person to actually follow through. Say what you mean and mean what you say. Actions do speak louder than words.

ॐ **Empty wagons make a whole lot of noise.**

Wagons carry food, grain, and anything that you haul on the farm. When the wagon is full, you don't hear any sounds. If the wagon is empty, it makes lots of noise. An empty wagon symbolizes someone who loves to talk but without any substance. In other words, when someone's talk is cheap, they are the same as an empty wagon making a whole lot of noise.

Corporately, the persons who generally do the most talking and complaining about meeting performance goals are the empty wagons. They spend valuable time explaining the reasons they haven't reached their goals instead of implementing new strategies to fill their wagons. Be careful of the empty wagons that are traveling beside you.

ॐ **You can't take back what's already out of your mouth.**

We've all had moments in which we've said something and wished that we could take it back the moment it came out of our mouths. I can also hear Granny saying, "Think before you speak." It doesn't matter how much you apologize; once the words are out of your mouth, the damage is already done.

ॐ **It's not what you say but how you say it.**

How you say something directly correlated to whether the other person even hears the message. For those of us, particularly women, who have very strong and direct voices, our messages are often misunderstood. A strong discerning voice is heard as a demanding voice to some and the message gets blown out of proportion. Being aware of this, I consciously strive to improve my communication style. The message may be warranted with constructiveness but if it is delivered in a harsh manner, perceived or not, the intended source blocks it out, leaving the true message unheard.

❦ **If you harvest thorns, look at your own garden.**

Thorns are like daggers. They may even have an abundance of sweet-smelling flowers surrounding them but they still hurt. This is a play on words as it is a reminder that we all have thorns. Thorns are seen as our habits and nuances of bad judgment. To keep our thorns from pricking other people, we need to constantly "tend our own garden" and work on self-improvement.

❦ **The grass is not always greener on the other side.**

There's nothing more beautiful than a well-manicured green lawn. When you're on the outside looking in, things may always look better in someone else's household, on another job, or in another situation. When you aren't privy to all of the facts, looks are deceiving. Only when you decide to make a move and enter into one of life's transitions, you realize that the situation you left was better than the one you're in. Evaluate carefully your every move when contemplating making a change. Decisions based on appearances alone can result in grass growing so wild, you'd need a new lawn mower.

⚘ **If you think the grass is greener on the other side, go ahead and buy you a new lawn mower.**

To buy a new lawn mower means that you were forewarned of the risks and consequences and you decided to do it anyway. If you are convinced that you need to move forward with a decision, be prepared to suffer the consequences of your actions. Your decision may cost you more than money, even a lifetime of regret.

⚘ **To belittle is to be little.**

To belittle is to purposefully speak demeaning words in an attempt to increase your own ego, which simply shows insecurities. People who are comfortable with themselves don't have to belittle others in order to build themselves up.

⚘ **You never know what's going on behind closed doors.**

You can't see what's going on in someone else's house, business, or life. This is a lesson on contentment, being satisfied with your station in life. Growing up, we didn't spend the night over at anyone's house unless it was a close relative. One of the reasons given was that we didn't know what went on behind someone's closed doors. This was a means of protecting us from growing up too soon and being exposed to many of life's issues prematurely.

Financially, we have recently seen millions of Americans trying to peep behind closed doors, living above their means or high on the hog, only to be bitten by the debt crisis. The one-time delicacy of the hog has turned distasteful, into a life of pain and discomfort. The misery of shattered lives, record foreclosures, and loss of retirement funds is the price our country is paying because of discontentment. It has proven that we really don't know what goes on behind the closed doors of others.

⚥ **A dog that carries a bone will bring one.**

Carrying a bone means to gossip or share something told to you in confidence. When you find someone who habitually spreads rumors or confidential information to you about someone else, rest assured they'll share your confidential information with others. When people trust you, they share with you very intimate details regarding crucial life-impacting matters. When you break that trust by carrying a bone, i.e. their confidences, you breach that trust just as you break the seal on a jar of your favorite jelly or jam. The ingredients are sealed to preserve the flavor. Preserve your trust and confidence.

⚥ **Let sleeping dogs lie.**

When a dog is asleep and you wake him up, he can become vicious and outraged. You may be subject to be attacked or bitten. To let sleeping dogs lie means to leave the past in the past. Things that happened yesterday are done. Once reconciliation occurs, it's unproductive to keep bringing something up. Forgiveness and letting go also have their rewards. When people died in the community, this is when you would learn how many children they may have had out of wedlock or the "juicy stuff" they did when they were younger. It always amazed me that folks would wait until someone died for all the sweet, juicy gossip to ooze out. When the information at hand has the ability to cause more harm, hurt, and damage than to edify, it's time to "let sleeping dogs lie."

⚡ A bird in the hand is worth two in the bush.

A bird in the hand is worth two in the bush means to enjoy the blessing you already have instead of risking it for what you think might be better. What you have is probably twice as good. What you already possess in your life or business is the "bird in the hand." The possessions you're seeking, sometimes greed, a calculated guess, or inherent risk, is the "two in the bush." Ever heard of someone with a fortune losing it all by one last gamble? All of their accomplishments could be lost by risking just one more chance for more.

⚡ You're jumping out the frying pan into the fire.

This is a wise warning to think carefully about getting out of a bad situation to end up in one that's twice as bad. The problems we inherit may be extinguishable in the frying pan but if we decide to jump prematurely, we could end up consumed in life's fiery path. When forced into quick decision-making, always play the "what if" game, weighing thoughtfully and prayerfully your options.

⚡ He who carries the cross carries the burden.

When you make a conscious choice to take a burden, grave concern, responsibility, or decision that another has made and place them on your shoulders, you have decided to carry their cross. Loading everyone else's problems on your shoulders is dangerous. Sometimes, it's just not your cross or problem to bear. Some people love for you to take on their problems so that they don't have to worry about solving them. If you continue to carry them, they will certainly allow you to do so. The burdens ultimately could have so much weight that it causes stress, emotional eating, and many other unhealthy issues. Carrying your own cross is a heavy load for your shoulders; adding everyone else's is not only a burden but simply overload.

֍　**That's not your cross to bear.**

Bearing the cross of others and owning their problems is a form of rescuing: rescuing them from problem solving, strategic thinking, and from reaping what they have sown. As a parent, it's sometimes easier to rescue our children but when you do so, it robs them of the joy of maturity. As a business leader, developing leadership is more about helping someone execute their VISION and not trying to develop the VISION in their heart.

֍　**If you can't say nothing good about somebody, then don't say nothing at all.**

Saying nothing at all is simple wisdom that can save your life in multiple ways. As mentioned earlier, Granny said that you can't take back what's already out of your mouth. We've all been guilty of this and have regretted it. During these times, when you are in a situation, breathe and listen. Resist the temptation. Silence may just tell it all.

֍　**Foxes have holes.**

The biblical implication is found in Matthew 8:20, which says, "Jesus said to him, 'the foxes have holes and the birds of the air have nests, but the Son of Man has nowhere to lay his head.'" (KJV) As we travel through our daily walk, it is not always about us. Our purpose is to deny ourselves and come to the aid of others who have a deeper need. It is about providing comfort, shelter, and a source of strength for the relationships that we have developed. When someone is in need, don't be like a fox, running into a hole, seeking shelter to cover up or scattering your nest. Since history repeats itself, you may soon be the one who needs the fox to come out of his hole to your rescue.

❧ **A hint to the wise is sufficient.**

When one has discernment, maturity, or a wise spirit, all you have to do is just give them a hint about something in order for them to understand or at least begin to put the pieces of the puzzle together. Leaders at the top of organizations are often guilty of not listening to folks on the bottom rung. These are the team members who "know all" yet everyone fails to ask them. When you're too far at the top, you're often the last person to know the causes of a potential downfall because your direct reports tell you what you want to hear, leaving out the most important details. A hint is a potential casualty that is sufficient for the wise.

❧ **When you know who you are, you don't have to waste time trying to be somebody else.**

When you know who you are, you're authentic, not trying to imitate others. When you mature to a point in your life and in your business at which you are comfortable with who you are and your convictions, it's a place of solitude and peace. You're not concerned with trying to please everyone. Strong leadership at home and work takes strength. When hard decisions have to be made, someone won't be happy. Being a people pleaser and doing the right thing are not always congruent. That's why you are *A Chosen Seed*. There are many seeds but few are chosen. *Chosen Seeds* are real and full of compassion and empathy. When you know who you are, you don't have to waste precious time being someone else. Being the best authentic you is more powerful than a great fake of somebody else.

❧ **We are all manufacturers—making goods, making trouble, or making excuses.**

When you manufacture something, it begins with a process and a desired intention. How you begin your manufacturing process is a good indication of the quality of your end result. Applying this to your life, ask yourself, "Am I/we making goods, making trouble, or making excuses?" Business cultures are not exempt from this exercise. A great strategy is to anonymously survey your staff and client base. Have them give you three grades: one on making goods resulting in excellent service, one on making trouble, and one on making excuses.

❧ **Excuses are nothing but justified lies.**

To justify is to have an internal belief about something, whether it is true or not. Justifications are often excuses for the truth. We can make excuses or try to justify but it doesn't change the truth. No matter how you spin it, justify it, or turn it around, the truth remains the truth. Being in the financial industry, I've heard some of the most polished, eloquent excuses imaginable. People on the outside of the financial walls make excuses about why things are the way they are while people on the inside are encouraged to justify the same. When you examine the situation with a microscope, the excuses and justifications are both a farce. Excuses are nothing by justified lies.

᷾   **Making excuses don't change the truth.**

Excuses are defense mechanisms to disguise the truth. All the explaining, blaming others for your mistakes, or diverting the reasoning to others are piled up disguises. No matter how you spin it or how glorious the excuses are, the truth still doesn't change. Instead of prolonging it, deal with it. It is what it is!

᷾   **If it sounds too good to be true, it probably is.**

While everyone has heard this many times, we have to ask ourselves, "If we know this, then why do we find ourselves being gullible time and time again?" Scammers and defrauders make their living giving you excuses, justifying ways to get you to buy into a get-rich-quick scheme or swindle you out of hard-earned dollars. These justified lies are means to victimize. If they can convince you, then they don't have to work hard for money. They just need to concentrate on working hard to obtain yours. Always read the fine print and take the time to think, pray, and review your options. I shared with someone recently, when they were trying to convince me to make a purchase over the phone, "If this is a one-time opportunity only for this phone call, then God doesn't intend for me to have it. If it's a great deal, then it should be available tomorrow." When something sounds too good to be true, practice saying one of the shortest but most potent words in the human language: NO.

> ❦ **If you don't stand for something, you'll fall for anything.**

To stand for something is to have boldness, especially when you know something is wrong or your heart says that it simply is not right. It's credible to stand up for the underdog or to challenge the status quo. Just one reminder: stick to the facts. That's how changes are made, laws are enacted, and integrity and strength of character are built.

During my banking days in the 80s and 90s, if you were an advocate or a pioneer, you had to take a stand, not only for yourself but for others. During my early days in commercial banking, when both women and minorities were nonexistent, if you didn't take a stand, you would be used as a doormat; predators were lurking for a new spot to step all over you. As a pioneer, it was my servant-hood to advocate for other women and minorities. When supervisors failed to provide them with individual training, I conducted credit memo writing and financial analyses reviews in my home, during weekends or on Sunday evening. I owe a great deal of my commercial lending and business success to Bonnie Hill, one of the first female commercial banking managers in the history of the First Union National Bank (now Wells Fargo). Standing up for others is the most incredible gift that a pioneer can pass on.

> ❦ **You can't straddle the fence.**

Straddling signifies indecisiveness. Continuous indecisiveness breeds fear of responsibility. To straddle the fence is to be noncommittal on an issue. Even when it's unpopular or people disagree with you, make a decision. People who straddle the fence are often untrustworthy. They will agree with everything, telling you one thing and me another. Indecisiveness and straddling the fence are a dangerous position.

֍ **If you sit around waiting for your ship to come in, you might miss the boat.**

A ship refers to an often missed opportunity. Missing the boat means that the time to take advantage of an opportunity has passed by. People that sit waiting for their ship to come in are usually poor planners, undisciplined, or have a slack worth ethic. They not only miss the boat but when opportunity comes; they may even find themselves sitting at the airport instead of on the docks of the marina.

֍ **Nothing beats a failure but a try.**

Failing is to stop trying. A great example: after thousands of failed tries and attempts, Thomas Edison in 1879 invented the commercial incandescent lamp. How would your life be impacted if over 130 years ago, he decided to not continue day after day to reach his goal? In life, all of us are ultimately in sales. After multiple failed tries, the next "yes" could be your most profitable relationship. Since the mind is a powerful tool, just tell yourself: "I didn't fail. I just discovered many ways that something didn't work."

֍ **Hard work ain't never killed nobody.**

Hard work is sometimes back-breaking. This was said usually during tobacco season, which is tedious and very hard work from sunup to sundown. This psychology was fuel to keep you going because you knew that it had to be done. The only choices we had were hard work and more hard work.

❧ The grave is full of great ideas.

The grave is a resting place for many grandiose ideas and visions not yet accomplished. Many people die having great, unfulfilled ideas either not executed because of fear, not being willing to put the elbow grease into getting it done, or being just plain lazy. Some may not have had the resources or committed the time to fulfill great ideas while others may never be willing to put forth the hard work, planning, seed sowing, and execution to bring them to fruition. My sister, Andriea Gamblin, repeated this adage in passing one day and didn't realize the impact that it made in me completing this book. For those of you reading this, this is your season. Take your ideas and execute them. What's stopping you from watering your vision seeds? Feed your spirit with a strategic plan and make it happen. Begin by putting one foot in front of the other. Since tomorrow is not promised, please don't take those great ideas to the grave. Nothing beats a failure but a try.

❧ Don't try to keep up with the Joneses.

"The Joneses" refer to people who seemingly have it all: money, material possessions, no troubles, and no bills. What a joke. Don't try to keep up with the Joneses is a message to live beneath your means! Growing up on a farm, we didn't realize we were poor because everybody around us had the same simple but joyous lifestyle. Keeping up with the Joneses warn us about growing up, making it, and developing a flashy lifestyle. We were cautioned that when we "got grown," i.e. came into adulthood, we shouldn't be so eager to acquire material things just because someone down the street has them. The best way to go broke was to covet what others had and not be able to afford it. This is almost eerie considering what has happened in our country the last four years. Keeping up with the Joneses is a prism to the current economic and financial crises.

> **Live beneath your means.**

Reeling from the financial and economic crisis that began in 2007, millions of Americans are feeling the results of not heeding to this old wise tale. Living beneath your means positions you for the unexpected that comes in all of our lives at one time or another. Living beneath your means gives you purchasing power. The current real estate market presents opportunities for people to maximize their investments. People who have savings for down payment funds and great credit can take advantage of an incredible real estate market, buying low and creating wealth.

> **By the time you can make ends meet, the ends might move.**

My mother, Carnell Troy, remembers this inspiration. When ends meet, they have the capacity for either side to move, from left to right or from front to back. When one does not live beneath their means, their goal is to make ends meet, not realizing that the ends can move. As our country absorbed the unemployment crisis, foreclosure crisis, and mortgage crisis, all of a sudden, the oil spill in Louisiana happened. The executives of BP as well as the country were caught off guard in total shock and panic. It cost billions of dollars to clean up, and the aftershock may be felt for many decades, compromising the ability to make ends meet and the livelihood for business owners and the families of the Gulf Coast for generations to come. The moving of these ends not only cost money but no price tag can be placed on the loss of life and subsequent health and environmental concerns.

❧ **You have to have two things to make a good marriage. You gotta find the right person and you gotta BE the right person.**

While this was referring to a marriage of husband and wife, it is applicable to any relationship. Whether it is work related, serving on a board, being on a sales team or performing community service, *YOU* are the common denominator. You have to be the right person in the right situation in order to develop win-win relationships.

❧ **When trouble comes your way, you must be doing something right.**

Troubles coming your way were actually seen as a positive sign because it meant that you were attempting to do something good or constructive. These tests produce patience and a stronger, more fertile *Chosen Seed*. It was instilled in us that "the devil don't mess with you unless you're doing something good." We should count it all joy when life throws a curveball. These curveballs will teach us lessons crucial to winning the ever-changing game of life. Those who lack trials and tests lack the stamina to endure until the end.

You don't ever want to be sidelined when the opportunity for the winning shot is scored, else your winning pursuits fade away. You are guaranteed to miss all of the shots that you don't take. So the next time trouble comes your way, congratulate yourself. You're doing great things.

❧   **No problems, no progress.**

With progress comes a certain amount of problems. In order to grow, mature, develop, and increase your value, your cultivation will be interrupted with some kind of unexpected situation. These problems are simply snags that come to light that will let you appreciate the journey, building strength sometimes as strong as an ox. Proverbs 14:4 says, "Where no oxen are, the trough is clean; but much increase comes by the strength of an ox." A little disturbance is both healthy and necessary. Just know that when you have problems, progress is taking place.

CHAPTER 3

Watering

• • •

Water is the most essential nourishment for all things, including seeds, humans, and animals. Nearly 70 percent of everyone's body is made up of water, which provides nourishment for survival. Research has shown that a person can survive as long as thirty days without food but under a week without water.

There are many reasons that water is necessary:

❧ Increases energy

❧ Minimizes the risk of certain cancers

❧ Flushes out waste and bacteria

❧ Moisturizes

❧ Promotes better circulation

❧ Provides a glow

The wisdom sayings in this section are nourishing to your body, spirit, and soul. They will provide a glow to your life while helping you to flush out the waste that will create havoc.

Nourishment
• • •

> ✌ **You don't miss your water until the well runs dry.**

If you've never tasted well water, you have missed a treat. With such a unique taste, it quenches your thirst like none other. Water is defined here as one's most prized possessions and valuables. The well running dry denotes what no longer exists. Water is symbolic of life or a person. The well running dry may be when someone dies or leaves for some other reason. This is a powerful lesson on appreciation and valuing the people and things in your life. We would often hear this after a funeral: visions of family members publicly expressing their love and affection to the deceased but not seeming to show that love while the person was alive. Out of habit, the people for whom you do the most may be the ones to take advantage of you. We don't tell them we love them enough and more importantly, we don't show them.

In business, some leaders wait until their best performers resign in order to appreciate their contributions to the company. When they threaten to leave or things go awry is when their worth is acknowledged. We all need to make a special effort to appreciate family, friends, and colleagues daily. Relationships are all that we have. Taking our relationships and employees for granted is a sure way to have a dry well.

> ✷ **Your mouth is full of deep waters.**

Flowing from our mouth, our words have the ability to be a river of hope or a fountain of despair. Because our mouth is full of deep waters, we have to constantly discern its purpose, ensuring positive nourishment. To put this in perspective, the average depth of the ocean is about 14,000 feet. The deepest trench in the ocean is 36,200 feet, almost seven miles. This *Grannyism*™ is a warning to be careful what comes out of our mouth, because once it's out, you can't take it back. Spoken words can cut with miles of deep hurt or soothe like a calm river to elevate one's spirit. Proverbs 18:4 says, "The words of a man's mouth are deep waters; the fountain of wisdom is a flowing brook." People who are wise speak because they have something *of value* to say. Fools speak because they have to *say* something.

> ✷ **You can't appreciate the sunshine until you've had some rain.**

Sunshine in life is a glowing ray of hope filled with beautiful promises. Rain is symbolic of a storm or cloud that comes into our being. After the rain and storms in our personal and business life pass, precipitation lingers. This precipitation, whether it's death, stress, an accident, or other tragedy, brings a greater appreciation for the things that really matter. The rain definitely puts priorities into the proper perspective. My father, Bennie Ledrew Shird, told me after I broke my ankle, that "in every season of life, some rain will fall." I definitely appreciate the sunshine of my strong ankle muscles more today than the previous five decades.

❧ **Don't rain on other folks' parade.**

This means applying negativism to a situation. Spoken words can elevate or drain dreams. Particularly if they are making small steps to progress, don't rain on their parade. Multiple singles in life can be more advantageous than a homerun. If one hits a single, chastising them about why they couldn't hit a homerun may discourage them from trying at all. Instead of raining on someone else's parade, build another float of your own.

❧ **All the dirt will come out in the wash.**

An all-day task, washing on washboards takes time, as you must make sure that the clothes are clean by washing them multiple times. Dirt is an analogy of deception and manipulation. The purpose of washing clothes multiple times was to make sure that they were squeaky clean, as like-new as possible. If it seems that certain people always get away with dirt, just give it some time. In time, the truth will be revealed. When it comes out in the wash, the deceptive and manipulative behaviors will be shown. What doesn't come out in the wash will come out in the rinse—meaning just give it a little more time.

❧ **Don't throw the baby out with the bathwater.**

Of course we didn't throw our babies out with their bathwater. To throw the baby and the bathwater out together means you're throwing away the sin and not the sinner. As we discipline our children, we detest the behavior, but continue to love and embrace them individually.

Relating this in business: if you're forced to downsize, perhaps instead of closing the entire department, hold on to those employees and best practices that could be revenue generators if given another opportunity. We all have faults, but life is fuller when we concentrate on the strengths of our relationships.

❧ Blood is thicker than water.

Blood is essential to life. It transports oxygen and other nutrients throughout our organs to regulate our bodies and defend us from infections. This adage means our family ties, family bonds, and relationships come first. The reference is about protecting and defending those who are connected by bloodline. While there may be sibling and family rivalry, when it comes to protecting and providing for their best interest, you do whatever it takes to sustain the well-being of loved ones. One should be able to call on family for help when no one else is around.

While everyone scatters all around the country, there is an imbedded peaceful spirit assuring that you have others who have your back and will throw out a lifeline. In Granny's era, she meant this in relationship to blood relatives. As you mature, there are long-lasting relationships developed over decades that inherently are as thick as blood. If you're blessed to have such relationships, cherish them.

❧ A little fire can kindle a big forest.

To kindle is to fuel a fire or cause it to burst into flame. A forest is a large wooded area full of trees and may even contain a stream, lake or river. Fire is a reference to anything that can cause havoc, usually the tongue. In other words, the words that you say can wreak havoc and can fuel a huge territory. What begins as a little fire has the capacity to burn a mighty forest. It also has biblical connotations in James 3:5-6: "Even so the tongue is a little member and boasts great things. See how great a forest a little fire kindles. And the tongue is a fire, a world of iniquity. The tongue is so set among our members that it defiles the whole body and sets on fire the course of nature."

❦ **A burning fire is better than a flame not yet lit.**

A burning fire is a stressful situation at hand. If the fire is already burning, you know the location and you've assessed the situation. You can devise a strategy to extinguish it. A flame not yet lit is the problem that you're anticipating. This adage means to concentrate on the burning fire or the problem that you have now instead of worrying about the things that have yet to happen. Most of the things we worry about never happen.

❦ **You can't see the forest for the trees.**

This means being in denial or simply clueless about a situation. This has enormous costs, especially when we have the experience and maturity to see that we're being taken advantage of. Sometimes we don't see the forest for the trees because we choose to be naive and in denial. With reflection, all of us have had some forest moments even when the tree was standing right beside us.

❦ **Worry is a mental tornado.**

A tornado is violent, a powerful gust of wind and rain often circling around. If you are in constant distress and worry, it will affect your mental state to the point that you lose all effectiveness. Instead of allowing worry to stampede your mind, breathe and pray!

- **Don't worry about tomorrow. Today has enough trouble of its own.**

We can't do anything about something that has not occurred. Remember, worry is a mental tornado. Instead of worrying about what tomorrow might bring, focus on the full-time job of handling the troubles of today. There is credence, however, in being proactive instead of reactive.

- **Worry is like a dog chasing its own tail.**

Can you visualize a dog going round and round in circles chasing his own tail? Worry produces the same effect, particularly if you're worrying about something beyond your control.

- **An ounce of prevention is worth a pound of cure.**

It takes sixteen ounces to make a pound. If you take small steps each day to avoid a catastrophe, it liberates you from the money, time, and energy it takes to fix it. This teachable moment is about procrastination. Don't put off for tomorrow what you can do today. Actually, as you age, if you don't do it today, you may not remember it tomorrow.

- **People that don't ever do more than they get paid for, never get paid for more than what they do.**

This is one of the best customer service statements, which can give anyone a competitive edge and will certainly elevate you ahead of the rest. Doing a little more than you get paid for, more than the customer expects, is a great relationship builder and revenue sustainer. *Relationships* are driven by doing more. *Transactions* are when you only do what you get paid for. Your future is dependent upon going above and beyond.

ᵹ **People who are easy to please are hard to satisfy.**

While satisfying and pleasing are very similar, to satisfy is to bring *extra* gratification and fulfillment. Let's say, the difference between good and better; or better and best. If people are easy to please, it takes extra effort to satisfy them.

In business, pleasing your customer is executing a good transaction. Exceeding a customer's expectations satisfies, keeping them coming back time after time. These multiples produce long-lasting relationships and ongoing revenue streams.

ᵹ **Do all things without murmuring and complaining.**

In her early years, one of the most admirable visions is Granny carrying a smile, humming a spiritual during situations so stressful that would make people today jump off a bridge or fall into a depression. A positive attitude makes a difficult job appear just a little more attainable. Without murmuring and complaining, she was convinced that trouble wasn't going to last always. Folks who were always murmuring and complaining were compared to winners and whiners, success and failure.

Philippians 2:14-15 reflects, "Do all things without complaining and disputing, that you may become blameless and harmless…children of God without fault in the midst of a crooked and perverse generation, among whom you shine as lights in the world."

❧   **It's easy to spend someone else's money.**

We negotiate church financing projects and I am amazed at how decisions are made in expense control or lack thereof when it comes to spending money that isn't ours. As children, we could always make more frivolous spending decisions if the funds were coming from a relative, but if it were our own money, we would carefully and methodically rationalize every penny. Adults are no different. If you are honored to be *A Chosen Seed* to invest and handle the finances of others, cherish that gift and be a wise steward over someone else's money.

❧   **How can you look at the speck in someone else's eye when you have a plank in yours?**

A speck is a tiny spot while a plank is a thick piece of lumber, usually bigger than a board. This lesson warns to be careful of throwing stones and criticizing others when you have bigger issues of your own. We would hear this in context to someone who would discuss openly the bad habits of somebody else's children, not knowing that their child was doing worse.

❧   **A hard head makes a soft behind.**

This relates to disobedience. If you're always making trouble and defying authority, then bad fortune is your reward. Wisdom can save you a lot of pain. Since all decisions have consequences, the aching pain could follow for an extended period of time.

✯   **If the shoe fits, wear it.**

This is a reflective and indirect way to give someone criticism or warning. People without wisdom and discernment may miss the meaning of what's being said. Instead of a hint, they may need a more direct approach.

✯   **Two can keep a secret if one of them is dead.**

If you tell a secret to two of your friends, it's no longer a secret. Rest assured, as long as they can talk, there's a high probability that it will be revealed. In other words, if you absolutely don't want anyone to know something, keep it to yourself, in silence.

✯   **Nobody knows your business unless you tell them.**

One of Granny's mottos was "What goes on in our house, stays in our house." It was her feeling that nobody else would be aware of your problems or issues unless you told them. This shocked me as a child because it's so true. Think about it: if you never told a secret, it would never spread. Look in the mirror when something spreads like wildfire.

This has a staunch comparison to intellectual property or business secrets: if you keep the news close to your vest, information is not revealed prior to you wanting it to be.

✯   **Silence is golden.**

Gold is considered to be a precious jewel, of great value and pleasing to the eye. Silence is golden is a priceless instruction. Its healing power is not only golden; it resounds for years.

❧   **Silence is healing for all ailments.**

When you have pain or a disease, you want to find an immediate cure. Restraining your lips in certain life situations may be the best cure for any ailment or problem that arises.

Proverbs 10:19 commands, "In the multitude of words sin is not lacking, But he who restrains his lips is wise."

❧   **The less said, the better.**

"Less is best" would serve us well in many walks of our life. Many experiences that we encounter would end up with a different outcome if we simply listened instead of speaking. People don't always want you to answer; sometimes they just want a keen and sincere ear.

❧   **Hold your piece and let the Lord fight your battle.**

To hold your piece means to be quiet, watch your mouth, and guard what you say, not letting others know you possess certain information. When we were told to "hold your piece," we usually were told something in confidence that was said about us. We were warned not to lash out at the other person, as this was a lesson in knowing exactly what others thought with the true character of the person revealed. By maintaining silence, with time, the truth will bolster like a fierce wind. That's when you know that the Lord fought your battle. This has proven to be a lifesaver, as you can discover the realness of people by merely sitting back and observing. When you find yourself in a situation that is spiraling out of control and appears to be as big as a giant, just hold your piece and let the Lord fight your battle. The battle is not yours, it's the Lord's. (I Samuel 18:47b)

> **Just because snow is on the chimney does not mean there's no fire in the stove.**

Snow is a reference to gray hair or age. Fire in the stove is wisdom. Never take senior citizens, employees that have been around for years, or any other seasoned individuals for granted. We can learn valuable lessons from their wisdom. While technology and change are great, nothing replaces the warmth of a burning fire that has been cultivated over time.

> **Every closed eye ain't sleep.**

My husband Ricky remembers his mom, Dora Boone Bennett, saying, "Just because someone's eyes are closed pretending to be sleep, does not mean that they cannot see." A closed eye also refers to people who lacked integrity or ethics, people who assume that other people are not aware of their actions and motives. Even when you don't think anyone is looking, there's always someone who is a witness to what's going on. With a camera on every cell phone, this applies to all walks of your life.

> **Every open eye can't see.**

We assume that if one has an open view of a problem, they could solve it. Not necessarily so. When open eyes are not focused, they're filled with paranoia and lack of vision, almost like zombies walking around not having a clear path. A great analogy is being in a forest full of trees so thick you have to carefully tread through, cutting a path as you rumble through the woods. What a miserable feeling.

❧ **Be careful how you live. Somebody's always watching.**

As we grew older we were expected to be role models for younger people in the community. The instruction was to be cognizant of your steps because someone was always watching your path. As leaders and parents, we never know who and when we are being watched. It seems that the candid camera is always clicking. Make sure your life can be emulated.

❧ **Everybody you meet knows something you don't. Learn from them.**

People come from all walks of life with different experiences and cultures. The lessons they can share are gifts. Unwrap these gifts and learn from every person you meet. There is a reason people cross our paths. Seize the opportunity to gain seeds that lead to abundance.

❧ **The blind are leading the blind.**

This means both the leader and the followers are clueless. The people in charge have less knowledge, experience, and know how than the persons they are responsible for leading. Without knowledge to accomplish a desired goal, both are going along haphazardly with no vision and focus.

- **You can't pour piss out of a boot, even if it's turned upside down**.

My brother, Arnie Troy, Jr., had an opportunity to live with Granddaddy Wiley Shaw. Granddaddy was stern and demanded discipline and perfection, even while cropping tobacco, plowing the fields, or planting the crops and seedbeds. When things were not done to Granddaddy's satisfaction and didn't exceed his expectation, this was his message. According to Arnie, when this was said, it was not a good day in the fields. In plowing the fields, the rows appeared to grow by a mile; he did his job over and over until Granddaddy was completely satisfied.

- **You ain't got a pot to piss in nor a window to throw it out of.**

The pot is symbolic of a lavish lifestyle or warped priorities. The window represents ownership. We heard this when people were spending money frivolously, living a lavish lifestyle or had their priorities out of order. The fourth Sunday in August is like a sacred holiday at Christian Plain AME Zion Church, our annual Homecoming. Everyone from the community traveled from around the world to come home and fellowship, dressed in their finest clothes and driving the best vehicles. Over time, it was discovered that many of the shiny cars were rented, only to drive home and profile. The men were especially impressed, until this discovery, giving the clear meaning of this *Grannyism*™. This financial principle is alarmingly applicable today. Lavish lifestyles have left many with no windows or pots.

ﬗ **You are like a fish out of water.**

Fish thrive best in their element: in the water where they can be productive and healthy. Like a fish, when you're out of your comfort zone, out of touch, out of sync with what's going on, this applies. Anytime you feel like a fish out of water, it's time to slow down, assess the situation and devise a new strategy. Water is survival. If the fish is out of water too long, it dies.

ﬗ **Don't rock the boat.**

This means to take caution in examining a situation before you make abrupt changes. What looks good from the outside may have an entirely different perspective when the alternatives are weighed.

Rocking one's boat means being close to falling into danger. When faced with any situation, you might consider being thankful and content that things are as well as they are instead of risking everything to ruin them. Things could be a lot worse. No matter how bad you think your problems are, there are others in a worse predicament that would love to trade places, as their problems are massive and more explosive.

ﬗ **You can lead a horse to the water but you can't make him drink it.**

Horses are stubborn, having to be led and prodded to perform certain tasks. In this saying, the horse is synonymous of a person and water is the nourishment of wisdom and advice. You may give repeated advice only to have it fall on deaf ears. As a leader or coach, it's a hard task to step back and allow others to feel the consequences of their actions. At some point, we become enablers instead of leaders or coaches. You can lead someone with constructive advice and wisdom, but if they fail to drink from the wisdom well, then dehydration and the effects of the dehydration can be deadly. We are all different and motivated differently. With some, you may point to the direction of water and they'll listen. Others stubbornly will hit their heads upon a brick wall, at which time the only course of action is to allow dehydration to run its course. Once you lead, move out of the way.

⚡ Don't ever let your left hand know what your right hand is doing.

Your hands are a guiding pair. This alert teaches to share some plans sparingly. Never share your vision too soon. When embarking on a project, use caution in sharing it with the wrong people or sharing it too soon. One reason people never reach their goals is that they allow others to talk them out of them, usually by someone who has no interest in your success or by someone who's never done anything significant. It's amazing that folks who have never done anything have all of the advice in the world. For example, if you're embarking on marriage, what value can someone who has never been married give you? Likewise, what wisdom seeds can someone who's never owned a business sow into your entrepreneurial goals? It's like rowing a boat from the shore.

In Matthew 6:3-4, this referred to being discrete when performing charitable deeds; never seeking public recognition.

"But when you do a charitable deed, do not let your left hand know what your right hand is doing, that your charitable deed may be in secret."

꙳ **That's a crying shame.**

A crying shame involves disgust, amazement, and astonishment. When anything happened that was unheard of or disgusting, Granny would say, "That's a crying shame," meaning how in the world would someone do something particularly to hurt someone else. To put this in context, when Granny was born in 1910, there were about 230 reported murders in the entire USA, so to harm someone or murder someone was "a crying shame."

꙳ **That's calling the kettle black.**

Kettles were black cast iron and could endure everything. When you had the audacity to speak ill about someone else and you were doing the same, it was calling the kettle black. It's the same as a hypocrite calling a liar a liar.

꙳ **You can either sink or swim.**

To sink or swim in an ocean is an inherent struggle. Some people would simply rather learn the hard way than to accept the advice from others. When you are insistent on defying constructive guidance, the elders would say, "he/ she will either sink or swim," meaning they would either drown, falling flat on their face, or their survival instincts would kick in and they'd swim to shore. Either way, it would be an unnecessary struggle.

⚡   **Faith without works is dead.**

Faith is strongly believing for something. Work is applying action. Granny sometimes referred to work as applying elbow grease to something, meaning you had to use your hands and knees as well as your brain to get it done. While you may have faith and truly believe your goals will be achieved, completion doesn't happen without a strong work ethic to accompany your desires. If you have a desired goal, you can't sit, hoping and waiting for it to happen. Without a little elbow grease, blood, sweat, and tears, faith without works is dead.

⚡   **A boat in a harbor is safe, but in time the bottom will rot out.**

A boat sitting safely in a harbor doesn't move to the next destination. Some opportunities come around only but once. To take advantage of yours, get up and do something to make a difference. If you just stand still nestled safe in your harbor, you may not be any good to anyone, and you may be rotting your bottom out. Ideas turn into visions but visions can't turn into reality without a well-executed strategy. Execution surpasses our fears, pushing us down the shore.

⚡   **Be the captain of your own ship.**

A captain navigates with precise caution and never begins a journey without directions, maps, and everything needed to steer with accuracy. Such is life. A ship refers to your individual or business life. We are all captains of our own lives and we have a choice every day as to how we navigate our paths. We can choose to have a strategic plan or we can make decisions once we're in the middle of the ocean. Poor planning and sailing without a road map will ensure turbulent waters with forceful waves tossing us violently, causing sea sickness.

A captain ultimately commands his/her vessel: he is responsible for safe and efficient operations, a leader in charge of accounting, payroll, inventory, compliance and security measures; a great captain is considered as a master of the sea. This is a great command for *A Chosen Seed* to take control and steer your own ship. When you allow others to take control, don't complain when you reach an undesirable destination of *their* choosing. Be the captain of your own ship!

CHAPTER 4

Nurturing

• • •

When you nurture a seed, you provide compassionate care, food, love, and anything else needed for it to grow and reach its fullest potential. Nurturing is deliberate and time-consuming, as it involves acts of kindness and selflessness.

These instructional pieces of wisdom not only nurture *Chosen Seeds* but foster encouragement that sustains and preserves personal and corporate values.

Nurture
• • • •

❧ **Look for the good in the bad.**

The good outweighs the bad, no matter how bad things are. When something seemingly looks like a bad situation, always look for the positive and the good that will derive from it. Businesses begin, healing occurs, visions are realized as a result of "bad situations," which light the fire that so many of us need to reach a desired goal. When I broke my ankle, my first inkling was, "Oh my goodness—the business. How are we going to manage?"

After much reflection, I've realized that breaking my ankle was a blessing. After working in the corporate world and building two businesses, I was oblivious to how really exhausted my body was. Being in a state of a rapid rat race, you don't realize the state of unconsciousness that you're in. This sabbatical, even with the pain, enabled me to reset priorities, value my family and relationships, as well as finalize a twelve-year goal of publishing this book. To look for the good in the bad is finding the bright cloud on our darkest day.

❧ **Charity begins at home.**

Our family is the most important gift each of us is given; it is our priority and first responsibility. Before you spend time, money, energy, and resources providing and caring for others, make sure that you're taking care of those at home. 1 Timothy 5:8 emphasizes that charity begins at home: "But if anyone does not provide for his own, and especially for those of his household, he has denied the faith and is worse than an unbeliever." Charity begins at home and then spreads abroad.

> **We are all a work in progress.**

A work in progress is like a tapestry. Don't ever give up on anybody or any seed. God performs miracles every day on the most complex and speckled seed. Woven with rich designs, we fulfill our purpose taking different paths.

> **Great timber grows on both trees and man.**

A source of revenue, heat, paper production, and furniture, timber is cut from the thickest woods. In order to grow great timber, the environment and other conditions all work together. Like the trees, timber in man produces a great harvest, full of fruit, strength, and value to serve.

> **The stronger the wind, the stronger the tree.**

Each of our bodies is considered a tree: a strong, towering vessel sturdy enough to weather the storms of life. Winds are problems, stresses, the ups and downs that make us stronger to withstand whatever comes our way. Know that the wind blows forcibly making you, the tree, stronger, fortified with reinforced strength to stand the tests of time.

> **Please and thank you never go out of style.**

As we go through changes in our lifestyle, cultures, and standards, we tend to forget the simple, most important things that got us where we are. Great manners never go out of style. Try it!

ॐ Don't look a gift horse in the mouth.

In farm life, horses were given as gifts. A younger horse is more valuable than an older one. You could tell the approximate age of a horse by its teeth. So this means if someone gives you a gift, don't try to look inside and determine the value; just be thankful and grateful.

ॐ Don't judge a book by its cover.

Judging a book solely by its cover is superficial because things are rarely as they appear. Some of the most valuable and precious gifts come in very small packages. Looks are deceiving so you can't judge people by what you see or think you see on the outside. Make decisions based on genuineness and facts rather than perceptions.

ॐ Don't spread yourself too thin.

To keep from spreading yourself too thin, you must learn to say NO. This is one of the smallest words in the human language but one of the most difficult to say. No matter the good intentions, over-extending yourself leads to ineffectiveness and a division of your efforts. Say yes to passionate interests which feed your spirit.

ॐ You can't burn the candle at both ends.

A candle represents your life. While a candle illuminates into beauty and light, it needs oxygen to make it burn. To burn a candle at both ends means that you're unfocused, doing too much without accomplishing or working too hard, often with little sleep.

  You can win the battle but lose the war.

This is a powerful relationship-building lesson. Losing a client over pennies is not worth losing a relationship, one that could result in hundreds of thousands of dollars over a lifetime. While you can certainly make money and build sales on transactions, building strong relationships can generate a lifetime stream of revenue and referrals. This is an astonishing win-win principle that should be embraced by all corporate teams.

  Spare the rod, spoil the child.

When you spare the rod, you spoil the child leaving them undisciplined. An undisciplined child will cause you pain. No one likes discipline but we all need it. Think if you had never been disciplined, what kind of person you would be. What kind of values do you think you'd possess? Undisciplined children grow up to be undisciplined adults. Undisciplined adults produce more undisciplined children. Undisciplined adults enter the workforce as undisciplined employees. Undisciplined employees are often promoted beyond their competence to undisciplined managers (notice we said managers, not leaders) with the cycle continuing and spreading throughout. Having worked with all types of people in many different settings, I know that discipline is love. The biblical implication in Proverbs 13:24 is very clear. "He who spares his rod hates his son, But he who loves him disciplines him promptly."

꙳ **Parents who want to train up their children in the way they should go, must first go in the way they want their children to go.**

A reflection of spare the rod, spoil the child, this instruction demands that we model the behavior that we're looking for in our children. As parents, we are like mirrors. The reflections we give become the reality to not only our children but others around you.

The business reference is profound: Business leaders that want to train up their employees in the way they should go, must first go in the way they want their employees to go.

꙳ **Life and death are in the power of the tongue.**

Our oldest sister Sadie McCoy remembers this one. The tongue is one of the most powerful instruments known to mankind. Life and death is a reflection of how great the impact of our speech and how it affects others. Proverbs 18:21 says, "Death and life are in the power of the tongue, and those who love it will eat its fruit." There is significance when the Bible emphasizes the word "death" first. Death is associated with harsh, sharp, and malicious words that can literally destroy one's soul and spirit. Encouraging, uplifting, comforting, and soothing words provide motivation to fulfill one's dreams.

꙳ **A quarrel starts out like a tiny hole with a trickle of water. If it ain't stopped, the trickle can become a flood.**

A meaningless quarrel has the potential to become a flood if it remains unresolved. A simple disagreement, miscommunication, or an insignificant quarrel can remain either insignificant or become devastating. An issue or conflict should be stopped before a dispute can even begin. Nothing should be allowed to fester to the point where it draws a huge wedge between relationships. In business, not addressing conflict can cost you millions in lost productivity.

❧ **Kind words turn away a fuss; harsh ones stir it up.**

The tongue of persons in authority can either put out a fire or heighten the flame by adding fuel to it. Proverbs 15:1 says, "A soft answer turns away wrath, but a harsh one stirs up anger."

❧ **You can't slide uphill.**

Sliding uphill is impossible. There is absolutely no chance of moving forward or excelling if your behavior and attitude are moving you in a backward direction. As you progress, some things and even some people have to be left behind. As you venture uphill, climbing the ladder to success, be aware that all of the onlookers are not supportive in seeing you at the top. They may be watching and waiting for the potential fall. Consistent continuous motion, one step at a time, is the only way to venture uphill to reach the top.

❧ **You've got just enough rope to hang yourself.**

When teenagers explore, the best decisions are not always made. They should be given just enough leeway to feel the consequences of their actions but not enough to hurt themselves. If you continued and were just hardheaded and did enough damage to feel like you're choking, that's when you felt as though you were hanging.

"A short rope will hang you quicker than a long one," is a version my husband Ricky was told, which has the same meaning. Ultimately, hanging yourself in life is awfully painful, no matter if it's a short or long rope.

❧ Don't go to bed mad with each other.

Older women gave this advice to young girls getting married. You were advised not to go to bed mad at your spouse because it would drive a wedge into your relationship. While easier said than done, it has true merits. Spiritually, Ephesians 4:26-27 says, "Be angry and do not sin, do not let the sun go down on your wrath." As it relates to business arrangements and marriages, allowing things to fester and lack of communication will divide the people while also driving a wedge to the bottom line.

❧ If you don't use your talents, you'll lose them.

Using your talents causes a refinement and leads on a path to expertise and accomplished skill. Do you know of someone who had a beautiful voice and stopped singing? Over time, if the skill is not honed, their voice seems to crack and the sound is never the same. Use the talents with which you were blessed to help your family, your colleagues, your community, and anyone to whom you can be of service. As in Matthew 25:25, whether you are blessed with five talents, two talents, or only one—use them because they will contribute to the beauty of the earth. Every good and perfect gift comes from above. (James 1:17)

⚡ **Something in the milk ain't clean.**

Milk provides nourishment for your body and is vital to grow strong bones. A white, distinctive liquid, milk is used in many ways. You can easily distinguish any kind of foreign object floating in it, even a speck of black pepper. No one wants to drink it if it has anything in it. When the milk is not clean, it's of no use; just throw it away. When someone continues to fill your mind and say things that don't seem real, perhaps they are lying or even dirty. Be careful because something in the milk ain't clean. My father, Bennie Ledrew Shird, shared this lying and deception lesson originally passed down from my Grandfather, Bennie Shird.

⚡ **I might have been born at night but not last night.**

When you gave tremendous excuses or shared unbelievable stories, this *Grannyism*™ was the response. If you gave constant excuses, trying to manipulate or deceive, you would hear this. In other words, "I've been there, done that, and heard that line before."

⚡ **When one door closes, another opens.**

A door is a symbol of an opportunity, often a promotion or new employment. Some of life's greatest rewards come after defeat or a closed door. Defeat has a way of allowing your mind to brainstorm and develop limitless strategies. When you're down, you have nothing to lose. You tend to weigh your options and charge ahead. Closed-door moments bring creativity, welcoming in new boundaries and wealth.

⚡ **A quitter never wins; a winner never quits.**

A most remarkable sight is watching how winners tackle a problem with intense persistence. A winner's most powerful weapon is his/her attitude. They never give up. Lorraine Stephens, a dear friend of mine, always has the most uplifting attitude. She could be enduring the biggest trial in her life and when you ask her how she's doing; her response is an overwhelming, "Wonderful." Winners go the extra mile and do the extraordinary things that quitters refuse to do. They always have gas in their spiritual tank and they never quit.

⚡ **Winners do what losers don't want to.**

Everyone seeks triumphant success but not everyone has the same drive or work ethic to realize their victories. It's simply sensational when you mull this over, as the separation between winners and losers is a very thin line. Take a moment, be honest with yourself, and assess the following:

- What seeds did you sow when no one else was looking or no one else knew about?

- What seeds were you sowing when your competitors were playing?

- What kind of attitude seeds did you sow that show gratitude?

- What seeds did you sow to challenge the process or the status quo?

- What seeds of coaching did you sow into another individual, colleague, or business without an agenda?

- What feedback seeds were sown in your life that you didn't accept as a gift?

- What seeds did you sow that unselfishly served others?

- What seeds of passion are evident in your sowing?

- What relationship seeds did you sow that will generate revenue for years to come?

Since this is a self-assessment, what is the grade that you give yourself, your business, your organization, or religious entity? No one can change the results but you. All of these seeds lead to winning and passionate service. The harvest is waiting. Winners do what losers don't want to.

CHAPTER 5

Fruitfulness

• • •

Every *CHOSEN Seed* has both the capacity and potential for fertility and to bear much fruit. Fruitfulness can be inviting, tempting, mesmerizing, appealing, and fascinating with beauty.

When you have gone through all of the stages and you are now bearing fruit:

- you've had a strong foundation with fertile soil and strong seedbeds

- you've been planted and stand tall and firm over the test of time

- you've been watered, by rain and by tears

- Compassionate nourishment has nurtured every root of your seed

Fruitfulness is a bridge to abundance. This collection of *Grannyisms*™ affirms, instructs, challenges, and gives appreciation of beauty from our fruitfulness.

Enjoying the Beauty
• • • •

  You can tell a tree by the fruit it bears.

You've never seen an apple tree that bears peaches or pears. You expect the apple tree to bear apples and a peach tree to bear peaches. In this analogy, *you* are the tree. The fruit that you bear will be congruent to the type of tree that's growing in your orchard or your life.

If you want to know what kind of fruit you are bearing, ask your children. If you'd like to assess what kind of fruit your business is bearing, ask your human capital.

  A fig tree don't bear olives.

This instruction breeds authenticity. In infinite wisdom, there is only one YOU that was created. Trying to camouflage and be someone else dilutes the real person that you are. Be the best YOU that you are purposed to be. Let your words and speech be a testament of your authenticity.

The biblical implication is found in James 3:12: "Can a fig tree, my brethren, bear olives, or a grapevine bear figs? Thus no spring yields both salt water and fresh."

  Don't run after what's for you. If you live right, it'll run after you.

  Don't chase after your blessings.

Running after life's blessings or selfishly chasing them leaves one winded, grasping desperately for more. My mother, Carnell Troy, remembers this from Daddy. I really love it. I've seen colleagues who just run after and chase after their next promotion, sale, or deal without merit and it seems that they always fall short of the prize. Joyce Meyer has an eloquent way of saying the same thing, "Don't chase blessings. Instead of chasing after blessings, we need to chase after God. If we chase God, He will chase us with blessings."

Proverbs 13:21 says, "Trouble chases sinners, while blessings reward the righteous!" (NLT)

⚹ **Your reputation will travel more miles than you ever will.**

At the end of the day, one's reputation is all that one really has. The message is to be careful how you carry yourself and how you treat people because your reputation will travel farther than you physically would be able to. Many will know the quality of your contributions.

⚹ **Your reputation precedes you.**

Many years before computers, Internet, Facebook, Twitter, and all the sources of technology afforded to us today, the wise elders said that your reputation precedes you. Granny instilled in us that our reputation would get to a certain destination before our physical body would. It's astonishing that you can Google someone or a business and your reputation is all over the world while you're sound asleep.

⚡ **Be the salt that you are.**

Salt adds flavor to anything that it touches. It enhances the most luscious piece of meat and serves a great purpose. This *Grannyism*™ refers to being of such worth that you add spice, flavor, and enhancement to whomever you meet. In your business, the business principles and the human capital hired to carry out the company's vision and mission should be the salt to flavor your clients' needs. The directive from Matthew 5:13: "You are the salt of the earth, but if the salt loses its flavor how shall it be seasoned? It is then good for nothing but to be thrown out and trampled underfoot by men." OUCH!

⚡ **Keep doing good things for people and don't worry about if they ever find out.**

Our community was filled with missionaries-in-training who didn't realize it. When your deeds are heartfelt, genuine, and sincere, it doesn't matter if the recipient knows. When you did kind deeds for people, you were never allowed to talk about them. It was unimportant and we never gave a thought if the recipient was aware who had performed the task. It was Granny's feeling that if you were sincere in your giving, no one else needed to know. Being a pioneer in the banking industry, there are many that have been on the receiving end of my blessings. In most cases, I never shared with them that I was the spark that lit their candle. It was unimportant for them to know, for it was the right thing to do.

⚡ **Nobody hides a lit lamp under their bed.**

A lit lamp under a bed can't be seen. As *A Chosen Seed*, you can't grow unless you are planted. Just like a garden seed, you have no usefulness if you stay wrapped up in your pretty package. Your talents and gifts are wasted if you don't use them. Explore, try new things, and take calculated risks. We even get direction from Luke 8:16, "No one, when he has lit a lamp, covers it with a vessel or puts it under a bed, but sets it on a lamp stand that those who enter may see the light."

- **Don't stay where you ain't welcome.**
- **Go where you are celebrated, not tolerated.**

If you're in a situation where you know you're not welcome and your usefulness is gone, it's probably time to find another home. This is apropos in every walk of your life. Just as a year has four seasons, your life does too. Decide if this is the season to make a change. I've heard another saying very similar but more eloquent by an unknown author: "Go where you are celebrated, not tolerated." When you are simply tolerated, your gifts and talents are unappreciated and have little value.

- **Honor your mother and father.**

Honoring your parents was a command, not an option. This might as well have been the first of the Ten Commandments in our household. It was considered a sin not to honor your parents, grandparents, aunts, uncles, church leaders, other neighborhood parents, and anyone else in authority. Exodus 20:12 says, "Honor your father and your mother, that your days may be long upon the land which the Lord your God is giving you." If you made decisions that showed dishonor, the days were long and unhappy.

☙ **You ain't fully dressed until you put on a smile.**

An endearing smile was the ultimate accessory. Fully dressed in a tailored suit is only half dressed without a smile. When I grew up, everyone were amateur tailors, making clothing for special occasions, particularly Easter. One of the most important impressions as a youngster was the realization that even though we were poor, we were happy. We never went hungry and by today's standards, even Dr. Oz would give Granny and the other women in our community an A+. From the garden, we had fresh vegetables, ate homemade natural meals daily, and raised our own chickens, hogs, and cows. I suppose you'd consider it organic by today's standards. The pear, apple and peach trees provided us with the most delicious homemade cakes, pies, and cobblers in addition to being the source for our jams and jellies, which we enjoyed throughout the winter months. We snuck to taste Daddy's homemade wine; the fully loaded grapevines provided the best wine, unavailable by even the best of wineries. Our neighbor, Mrs. Mamie Spaulding, churned butter for those delicious homemade desserts and life was good. We had a reason to be fully dressed with a smile.

☙ **Give me my flowers while I'm living.**

Flowers are symbolic and show love and appreciation. Culturally, we have a history in our community of purchasing flowers when someone died. The funeral would be lined with hundreds and sometimes thousands of dollars worth of flowers. Granny and others would say, "Give me my flowers while I'm living so that I can see them, smell them, and enjoy them because when I'm dead and gone, I won't be able to see them or smell them."

The same goes with your employees: don't let them threaten to leave before you show love and appreciation. Give them flowers daily with a thank you and recognition. "Please" and "thank you" never go out of style.

ᵶ   **Slow down and smell the roses.**

A rose causes you to pause and breathe its aroma. Roses bloom for but a season and when the aromatic petals are gone, what's left is a rosebush. This adage means that you need to slow down, count your blessings, smell and enjoy the sensuous aroma. I've been oh so guilty of this so I can caution others: it's easy to be a passenger on the merry-go-round of life. You can spend all your time doing so much good for so many people that you forget to slow down and enjoy the fruits of your labor.

ᵶ   **When in doubt, do the right thing.**

If you have to think about what to do when faced with life's challenges, the choice is easy—do the right thing because it will shine back in your face sooner than you think.

Corporately, the decision is the same. While revenue is the lifeblood of every business, integrity is the blood transfusion to sustain you through the multiple stages of the business cycle. Do the right thing!

ᵶ   **Many people can see...but only a few know what they are looking for.**

My brother-in-law, Henry Terrell, a retired educator in Piscataway, NJ, remembers a colleague sharing this wisdom.

Some have twenty-twenty vision, but have blinders on that prevent their ultimate success structure because they have no clue as to what they're looking for. When building a financial or business strategy for a client, we often ask them, "What does success look like? What will you feel when we solve the financial dilemma?" What we're doing is painting a picture of their VISION on paper. Only when you explicitly define it, write it down, and make it plain will you be assured that the right road map is developed and being executed or followed. You have to be focused and know what you're looking for in order to know what it looks like when you see it.

ɤ   Knowledge is worth more than gold.

Gold is such a precious jewel; however, knowledge and education will afford you to break through unforeseen opportunities of gold. Having grown up on the farm, knowing the essence of a struggle and an incredible work ethic, Granny would always tell her children, grandchildren, and great-grandchildren, "Chillen, whatever you do, get your education." Knowledge through education was the boarding ticket and passport for a better life, worth more than gold.

ɤ   Close your mouth and open your ears. Opportunity knocks softly.

Opportunities are doors opening, allowing you to walk to your destiny. Opportunities are avenues to fulfill your purpose. We all have two ears and one mouth. We were told the reason God did this was for us to listen twice as much as we spoke. Only when you listen to HIS voice, can you discern the upcoming opportunity. Some of the most profound opportunities knock softly. Listening provides you the right positioning to take advantage of them.

❧ Let go of the past.

This is a path to freedom. The past can cripple you if you allow certain things to linger. Your past can cause a paralysis that will have you stuck in a rut. If left long enough, it begins to feel comfortable. Let go of yesterday, live for today, and cherish tomorrow.

❧ You can't cry over spilled milk.

Spilled milk is a parallel to yesterday's problems. When milk is spilled, it is out of its original container. There's absolutely nothing you can do about milk that's already spilled, anything that happened yesterday, or that happened in the past. Questioning why is unproductive and unhealthy. Now that yesterday is over, learn from it and implement changes so that unpleasant events don't reoccur.

❧ Beauty is but skin deep.

There are many people who look good and smell good on the outside. Only when you get close do you discover that the perceived beauty has a strong, distasteful, and smelly odor. The true beauty of *A Chosen Seed* is on the inside, not the outside.

❧ There are no degrees of honesty.

Unlike the weather, there is only one degree of honesty—the truth. Honesty is always the best policy and then you don't have to remember what you've said. When the truth isn't told, you have to remember exactly what you said, making a bad situation worse.

* **Fast money flies fast.**
* **Easy come, easy go.**

Simple, yet economically compelling, this lesson warns that if you gain money or wealth by deceit, lies, fraud or any dishonest means, it will dwindle away like sifted quicksand devouring its victim. To every kindergarten classroom to every boardroom to every pulpit, this message is screaming to be immersed in our hearts in this 21st century. Since there are no degrees of honesty, fast money flies like a silhouette of flocking birds migrating to the south for winter. Money gained by easy measures with dishonesty, go easy into the clouds; seeming to perish with the wind. Proverbs 13:11 is crystal clear: "Wealth gained by dishonesty will be diminished, But he who gathers by labor will increase." Steady diligence pays off!

* **You're writing your tombstone each day.**

An epitaph is a summary statement of a lifetime. Being *A Chosen Seed* is a difficult assignment. Every step and decision you make is relative to the writing of your tombstone. If yours were written today, what would it say?

In business, if you were in a succession stage, what would people articulate regarding your integrity? Were you more interested in dollars vs. human capital, profits over people, or relationships vs. transactions? The answers are written every day, providing the final epitaph.

ⵣ   **Leave everything a little bit better than you found it.**

Whether it was your responsibility, your job was to leave everything a little better than you found it. This applied to cleaning up the kitchen as well as the impact you made in your school, community, or place of employment. Wow, wouldn't it be a wonderful world if everyone took Granny's directive?

ⵣ   **Live life like an exclamation, not an explanation.**

This means to have fun, with excitement and not with excuses. Consider this exercise with your family, friends, sales teams, and employees: ask all participants to close their eyes, clear their minds, and write down the first three things that come to mind when they hear a certain person's name. Start with YOU. How would people describe you without you being in the room? Now analyze the results. Are the adjectives an exclamation or an explanation? You are the only person who has the power to change the outcome.

ⵣ   **Don't let other folks steal your joy.**

When you allow folks to do this, you give them a piece of your power. There are some people who will always try to pour water on your fire. When you're happy about a goal accomplished, a promotion, or a blessing and someone comes along who has something negative to say—don't let them steal your joy. Don't give your power away. No one can steal your joy or take your power without you allowing them to do so. Give yourself permission to maintain your joy and your power.

❦ **What you weave in time, you'll wear in eternity.**

Granny has always quilted and crocheted. Even today, when not in arthritic pain, she still crochets gorgeous works of art. At one point she wove baskets. Weaving takes patience and time. In this lesson, it represents how you live your life, impacting and sowing seeds of greatness. In time, after nurturing, fruitfulness occurs. The fruit that you bear will be rewarded in eternity, the ultimate reward.

❦ **More pain, more gain.**

Hard work comes with a price. The price may be a result of discipline, sacrifice, and prioritizing. You definitely have to endure a certain amount of pain in order to gain the desires of your heart. Getting to the top is an admirable achievement; just be careful how you treat people going up. A strong foundation will provide a source of strength as you travel upwards.

❦ **More gain, more pain.**

If you desire to have more, expect for the price to go up. When seeking the next promotion, carefully analyze whether the discipline, sacrifice, and reprioritizing is worth the gain. What looks grand may not be worth what you have to give up to get it. As you age, your priorities change, making it easier to discern the levels of both gain and pain.

❦ **The easy way is not always the best way.**

There are people who will always choose the easiest way to do something. While it may be the easiest, it may be more time-consuming and ultimately more costly. My husband Ricky remembers this one growing up. This is a timely lesson for leaders and sales teams today.

❧   **The apple didn't fall far from the tree.**

When apple trees were full of delicious fruit, as the wind blew, the apples fell on the ground very close to the tree. An apple represents your family, your heritage, and your gene pool. This was a warning on being in relationships with people who didn't have strong character and morals, especially if you knew who their relatives were.

Particularly when you started dating, the adults were leery of your friends if they thought that they were the product of a bad seed. In other words, if they knew something detrimental regarding the family, especially the parents or grandparents, they were reluctant for you to have close ties. They felt that by association, the children would develop the same habits as their family because the apple never falls far from the tree.

❧   **Who yo (your) people?**

This was an assessment of family values. One of the first questions Granny would ask any of my friends when meeting them for the first time was, "Who yo people?" It was important that she knew the family to assess what kind of stock they came from. I certainly thought this was cruel and nosy but after raising three very fine, professional, and collegiate young men, there's great credence in being aware of the influences and associations your children have. In the corporate world it's illegal to ask this question but it's masked by: "Tell me about your family," or "What core values did you learn growing up?" or "I'd love to get together for dinner with your family." While today's tactics are more politically correct and more eloquently asked, the outcome is the same.

⚡ **May the works I've done speak for me. May the life I live speak for me.**

This is an old Negro spiritual which is very sincere. In our community—Christian Plain AME Zion Church community—what you did for others wasn't intended to be shared with all. Your actions were genuine and no one looked for accolades or pats on the back for being a steward or servant. Some of the biggest hearts are found in the people of this special community. God will grant their reward. What a beautiful testimony and epitaph.

⚡ **It's not what you know but who you know.**
⚡ **It's not who you know but who knows you.**

Who you know can save your life. This teaches you the power of building, sustaining, and valuing true relationships. Relationships are everything. Just like your reputation, a relationship will carry you further and more quickly than you could ever imagine. Relationships are built with sincerity, without an agenda, through appreciating people when you don't need anything. A sustaining relationship is just calling to see how someone is doing instead of calling only when you need a favor. All of us have family and friends that we only hear from when they are in need. True relationships come to your aid without asking. A modern version acclaims: "It's not who you know but who knows you."

≈   **Even a cracked pot can be used.**

None of us are perfect; we are all cracked pots. Just because the pot is cracked you don't throw it away. You polish and clean it because age makes it better. Granny and others cooked with cast-iron skillets and pots. Cast-iron pots had multiple uses. The huge ones that weighed seventy-five to one hundred pounds would make food taste especially mouth-watering. They were used to boil water to wash clothes as well as cook the world's most appetizing meals, including fish frys and chicken bog made with chicken, rice, and sausage, seasoned to perfection. As years passed and all of the siblings moved out of the house, Granny had to find other uses for the pot. You'll never guess: She made lye soap in it, strong enough to eat away all of your skin. In earlier years, farmers and mechanics used lye soap to clean their hands thoroughly from tobacco stains, auto grease, and anything that was hard to scrub. Lye soap was also our Dove and Dial, washing you clean, clean, clean. While this may seem antiquated, none of us were plagued with skin diseases, rashes, or other dermatology needs. I'm sure the lye ate all of the toxins away. At one hundred years old, Granny has the most gorgeous skin. As Granny discovered ingenious and creative uses for the one-hundred-pound iron pot with multiple imperfections, so can we be used. As *Chosen Seeds*, choose to be of great servant-hood as an imperfect cracked pot with extraordinary value rather than a beautiful, empty container.

CHAPTER 6

Pruning

• • •

In order to encourage new, healthier growth and re-vibrancy, a plant needs to be pruned, or cut back. As *A Chosen Seed*, life sometimes cuts you down in order to bring more vibrant life. You realize successful establishment of your plans as the result of pruning lessons. Seemingly never on our time schedule, the lessons are deliberate, harsh but necessary for the seed's purpose to be fulfilled.

Pruning may be the result of moving certain people and influences in and out of our lives. People come in and out of our paths during seasons, with distinctive roles and purposes. Since Granny has been blessed with one hundred years of life, let's look at the seasons in her stages of age: she was born in March, so spring represents the first twenty-five years; summer to age fifty; fall to age seventy-five; and winter as the grand finale. Each time you have an experience during which life teaches you a lesson, that pruning experience is intended to strengthen you for your next season. Wisdom comes when you grasp the gift of learning and are poised to articulate it to others for the intended good.

I heard a pastor say years ago that "people are like scaffolds." Scaffolds are temporary structures used to support people and materials in the construction or repair of building and other large structures. They are usually a modular system of metal pipes or tubes, made of either steel or aluminum. The purpose of a working scaffold is to provide a safe place to work with safe access suitable for the work being performed. Safety standards have to be strongly adhered to because the foundation for which they are being used to support is not only essential but has to remain sturdy sometimes for decades, and in some cases, a lifetime. While the scaffolds have immense endurance and strength, they are temporary. So how do people correlate with scaffolds? We are intended to be of service, provide a safety net and a strong foundation for those around us—**temporarily.** As team leaders, coaches, teachers, parents, and even friends, our job is well done when people are strong enough to stand up without a prop. Sometimes we prop too long, which hinges into enabling. While it's true that people who cross our paths have an intended purpose, people will come in and out of our lives during different seasons. When your scaffolding job is done, quietly move out of the way and allow the individual to flourish and even sometimes fall. Wisdom and discernment will nudge you to know the right time. Pruning begins when you remove your steel transition. These *Grannyisms*™ prove that every *Chosen Seed's* life has scaffolding and requires pruning in order to fulfill its purpose.

Being Pruned
• • • •

❧ **Everything that bears fruit gotta be pruned.**

Granny always had beautiful flowers, a plentiful garden, and apple, pear, and peach trees in the backyard. Everything that had the potential to bear fruit had to be weeded, cut back, and nurtured in order for it to bear more flowers, fruit, and vegetables year after year. The same process takes place in our lives. *As Chosen Seeds,* being pruned does not feel good at all but it's necessary in order for our value, beautification, and worth to develop, both individually and in business. We all are vines and the ultimate vinedresser brings out the most luscious finished product. John 15:1-2 says, "I am the true vine, and my Father is the vinedresser. Every branch in ME that does not bear fruit, HE takes away, and every branch that bears fruit, HE prunes that it may bear more fruit."

❧ **Get rid of stuff that ain't bearing no fruit.**

When a tree or plant wasn't bearing any fruit, its value diminished. This was a play on words to live on purpose. Live purposely and have a purpose through your living. If something has no value, remove it from your daily practice to make a smoother path for your walk. This refers to relationships also. If they are not fruitful, you may want to consider leaving them in the past.

❧ God don't like ugly.

This is a staunch reminder that ugly behavior, habits, and actions are not pleasing. Being cognizant of your actions when no one else is watching, how you treat others, or sowing seeds that profit by greed are barometers of your services. When Granny and others repeated this, you knew someone had done something that was not pleasing.

Personally, the repercussions of this corporately and nationally are being displayed economically. The leadership principle is simplistic but powerful. Our current economic downfall was brought on by profiting from greed. You may escape the punishment for years but justice will eventually track you down. The unemployment statistics, bank failures, recession, sluggish economy, and foreclosures are all examples of "God don't like ugly." As a nation, we will reap what we sow, good and bad.

❧ Don't ever lessen the lesson.

As you contemplate the various experiences of life, some are disguised as gifts. Gifts that teach valuable lessons that will propel you to produce more bountiful fruit at a later time. We go through gifts of pain to benefit and enhance not only our lives but the lives of others. Don't ever lessen the importance of the lesson. Lessons are purposeful and intentional. Many times when persons are going through a wilderness experience, we blame Satan, giving Satan too much credit and power when it's God all the time giving us instructions for life.

❧   **Some people enjoy staying in hell 'cause they know the names of all the streets.**

When you know all the names of the streets in a community, you are very familiar with your surroundings. On the farm, pigs loved slop and would even wallow in it. They are well aware that it's slop and they enjoy the comfort of their surroundings. If your path has people who enjoy living in hell, comfortable and enjoying slop, a right turn at the next intersection would be appropriate. The streets of excuses, procrastination, hopelessness, despair, disobedience, selfishness, and misery do not bear any fruit. While trials and obstacles may prune your life, *A Chosen Seed* should always be growing.

❧   **People in hell want ice water.**

Dora Boone Bennett, my husband's mom, would impart this wisdom to her six children when they were demanding material possessions. After the premature death of Ricky's father, Clayton Soloman Bennett, his mom worked tirelessly to provide for her young children, ages four, five, six, eight, nine, and eleven. She was a cheerful giver, but when one of the siblings would passionately desire something frivolous instead of an absolute necessity, they would hear this message. If Ricky wanted a pair of name brand tennis shoes to play basketball instead of the cheaper, no-name brand, her response would be, "Well, people in hell want ice water too." Her main goal was to put food on the table and provide a roof over their heads.

This challenges you to carefully consider the desires in your life. Distinguishing between the wants and needs in life sets priorities. If we constantly desire our wants to be fulfilled, not taking into consideration the big picture or more pressing needs, then we're no better off than people in hell who made bad decisions and want ice water to cool them down.

> ❧ **If you lay down with dogs, you'll get fleas.**

Since dogs are roaming outside, they may get fleas lurking on their bodies. These fleas may cause much pain. This truth confirms that life is all about positioning and if you put yourself in a particular situation with the prior knowledge that it will be painful, potentially damaging, and harmful, then the consequences are well deserved. When compromising your values, you may attract an unwanted aftermath of pain.

> ❧ **Iron sharpens iron.**

Farmers and blacksmiths sharpened their own tools with iron. Iron is the only thing that can sharpen iron. This abundant lesson involves positioning and associating with people or groups of people who can enhance what you already have or have similar goals. Inspiring colleagues inspire others to be better. Accomplished colleagues inspire you to accomplish your goals. If you're a student, position yourself to be tutored by a scholar, not someone who's failing the same class. If you are contemplating entrepreneurship, seek out successful business owners. Someone who has never owned a business can't impart the wisdom needed.

Proverbs 27:17: "Iron sharpens iron, so a man sharpens the countenance of his friend, to show rage or worthy purpose."

- **Practice what you preach.**

This means to say what you mean but live what you say. As parents and leaders, it's difficult to tell our children or colleagues one thing if they witness us doing the opposite. Preaching is an accomplished skill but practicing what you preach is a modeled behavior.

- **If you make your bed hard, you'll have to lay in it.**

Lying in a hard bed is extremely uncomfortable. A hard bed represents consequences that are the direct result of prior decisions made. If you consistently make bad choices, ignore warning signs, and make decisions without fully analyzing situations, then you'll have to bear discomfort, lying and tossing in a bed of pain.

- **Don't expect people to listen to your advice and ignore your example.**

As a leader, if you fail to practice what you preach, you severely compromise your effectiveness to lead. If your team is expected to have integrity in business dealings with clients, then your integrity has to be modeled. Your modeling example is more powerful than all of the eloquent words you speak in your sales meetings.

- **Troubles don't last always.**

Whenever trouble comes your way, let it be an opportunity for joy as it tests your faith and perseverance, affirming that better days will come. When we are taught the lesson we're supposed to learn, then the tides will turn, resulting in peace and joy. "For when your faith is tested, your endurance has a chance to grow. So let it grow, for when your endurance is fully developed, you will be strong in character and ready for anything." James 1:3-4 (NLT)

⚥ Play with fire and see don't you get burned.

A burn can be blistering. After multiple warnings, if you move forward with a decision that you know is not in your best interest, you can expect intense pain. Have you ever told a child not to touch a burning hot stove and they did it anyway? Like a child, disobedient adults don't believe fire is real until they are burned.

⚥ You can't walk on coals and not get your feet burnt.

Walking on coals is risky. Some risk taking is healthy, but when you risk the safety and stability of others, you maximize the potential danger. We all have to take calculated risks but make sure you have a cushion, fluffy and strong enough to ease the pain and blisters.

⚥ Weeping may endure for a night but joy comes in the morning.

Weeping comes from life's challenges, trials, and tribulations. While no one likes to weep, everyone loves the feeling of joy. Life itself comes with its own share of stresses. These stresses come with their own share of tears. Possessing the right attitude, mindset, and positive demeanor will often determine how long you stay stuck in the weeping stage before you can enter into the joy stage. Even in despair, this is a great promise. Psalm 30:5 references: "For his anger endureth but a moment, in his favour is life; weeping may endure for a night but joy cometh in the morning." (KJV)

⚡ **What's done in the dark will eventually come to light.**

The darkness is likened to doing things when no one is looking. If you have malicious and deceitful habits, they will surface in time. People will eventually see the real person and discover the truth, usually at the most absolute worse time for the deceiver.

Deceptive business practices will ultimately be revealed, too. Take another look at the financial crisis. Loose lending practices, programs, and mortgage opportunities welcomed greed and fraud. It transpired over a period of years, but the downfall of major corporations crippled our nation with record bank failures and foreclosures. The BP oil crisis also comes to mind. If shortcuts were taken, safety compromised, and drilling procedures modified for revenue gain, the result of those shortcuts will imperil our society for years to come. The environmental impact and affects on the business economy may be felt for decades. Luke 8:17 says, "For nothing is hidden that will not be disclosed, nor is anything secret that will not become known and come to light."

⚡ **A leech only knows two things: Gimme and Gimme mo (Give me and Give me more).**

"Gimme" is the old folks way of saying "give me," describing what a person says who has greedy intentions and possesses a selfish spirit. A leech is a parasite, a bloodsucking worm that attaches itself and clings on its victim, often causing bleeding. In life and with a seed, a leech only wants its victim to give, continue to give, or be used and give some more. People who are leeches have inward and selfish motivations and feel very secure and comfortable in attaching themselves. The behavior is justified in their mind. Selfish-spirited and leech-spirited individuals always seem to go around and around in circles. Their accomplishments take twice as long to come to fruition. With a closed fist, nothing leaves their hands; yet they aren't savvy enough to realize that a closed fist blocks potential blessings from coming in. Proverbs 30:15 says: "The leech has two daughters: Give and Give. Three things are never satisfied; four never say, "ENOUGH."

ȣ **Pigs get fatter while hogs get slaughtered.**

We raised hogs from the little baby pigs to their ultimate size for slaughtering. Slaughtering hogs was a grand time because Daddy would hang the homemade sausage, bacon, and ribs in the smokehouse until the perfect timing. Perfect timing with Granny's yummy homemade biscuits was worth every second of the wait. So what's the difference in the pig and the hog and why did the hogs get slaughtered? Hogs were greedier; once they got to a certain weight, they became the next breakfast and dinner meal. Taking advantage of the pigs due to their smaller size by pushing them away from the feeding trough ultimately got them killed. When the hogs were loaded in the truck to be taken to the slaughterhouse, the pigs were in the corner feeling less full, but happy that they were small.

Greedy and selfish business and personal maneuvers will always end up defeating goals. Slaughtering in business turns into mergers, acquisitions, and loss of revenue and human capital. Slaughtering in business was the bridge to our current recession.

> **Don't bore people with all your problems. They have enough of their own.**

Daily applying all of your problems on someone else's shoulders is a heavy, even burdensome, task. While everyone needs a great friend, a listening ear to seek sound advice, some problems are best not shared; rather, we should work them out alone. For a diversion, meditate, volunteer your time helping the less fortunate, perform community service, or visit the elderly or sick. This will quickly put life in perspective.

> **Don't judge anybody until you've walked a mile in their shoes.**

This means having empathy and seeing life from another's perspective. Many are guilty of prejudging with no knowledge of others' circumstances. Unless you've been in the exact same position as someone else (and we usually haven't), then your judgment is without merit. When you're walking, a mile can be time-consuming and tiresome depending on the conditions around you. Unless you have the life experiences to compliment someone else's journey, then perhaps you need a new map.

> **If you don't like something in somebody, change it in yourself.**

Look within first. When you detest the flaws of someone else, search deep within to determine why they strike such a heavy nerve. If you have the same habits, modify them in yourself first. Looking within is a powerful agent of change.

℣   Experience is the best teacher.

Particularly in your youth, you would rather experience things for yourself. While experience is a great teacher, the price is sometimes steep, costly, and even devastating.

℣   If you ain't never had hard times, just keep on living.

When life is going flawlessly, we tend to make decisions based on today's conditions only, without considering the thoughts of a lurking crisis that may occur tomorrow. If you're fooled into thinking that you'll never hit a stumbling block, time will be your best teacher. Just keep on living.

℣   Ponder the path of your feet.

The body is an amazing and ingenious creation. Our feet take us wherever we want to go, whenever we want to go. If you walk without any consideration, the road can be quite treacherous, with evil lurking all around. Proverbs 4:26-27 says, "Ponder the path of your feet and let all your ways be established. Do not turn to the right or the left; Remove your foot from evil."

℣   It's time for you to be eating solid foods.

As a baby grows, he/she graduates from formula only, to cereal, and eventually to solid foods. Eating solid foods means you're not a baby anymore and should be producing better results from mature decisions. We were told this when we made an immature decision.

Companies can apply this when assessing the skill level of team members based on training and time on the job. The biblical reference is mind-boggling: Hebrews 5:12b-14 says, "You have come to need milk and not solid food. For everyone who partakes only of milk is unskilled in the word of righteousness, for he is a babe. But solid food belongs to those who are of full age, that is, those who by reason of use their senses exercised to discern both good and evil."

⚘ Anything that's dead need to be buried.

We heard this in church when no one was saying AMEN. Sunday was a day of praising God, being thankful for all of His blessings, and acknowledging how far He had brought the family over the last week. You were expected to be thankful by singing, praying, and worshipping. Worshipping was the source of your praise. When things got quiet, the Preacher would say, "Anything that's dead need to be buried." In other words, if you couldn't show the appropriate praise then you didn't deserve the blessing of just being alive. This was sometimes followed with, "If a robin can say thank you, you can do it too." This fact alone is praiseworthy.

⚘ If a robin can say thank you, you can do it too.

Sweet chirping and singing: if the robins and birds take the time each day to give thanks, then we should certainly take a quiet moment to show gratitude. Sitting on our front porch rocking peacefully, the robins and birds sing the most harmonious and entrancing music. They spread their wings and just chirp melodies of thanks, teaching impelling lessons.

The Mighty Clouds of Joy, a gospel recording group said it best with the chorus exclaiming:

> "Everybody ought to praise His name,
> Be thankful and praise His name,
> Everybody ought to praise His name
> 'Cause if the robin can say Thank You
> You can do it too."

- **If you can't stand the heat, get out of the kitchen.**

With no air conditioning, our kitchen stayed extremely hot during the summer months. This wisdom paralleled life's endurances to the heat in the kitchen. When you earnestly seek and ask for something and finally get it, you have to pay the price for what comes with it. Sometimes we ask and beg for things that aren't good *for* us, but good *to* us. This message is a test of strength to determine if we can make adjustments to better handle life's curves. So if you can't stand the heat or the pressure, then you may have to get out of the kitchen, admitting that the consequences are too much to handle. There is absolutely nothing wrong with admitting you have made a mistake. If what you are seeking is truly meant for you, then it won't be a struggle.

- **God won't put no more on you than you can bear.**

During the Desert Storm war in 1990-91, my brother and sister both were deployed to Saudi Arabia. Bill (aka Willie Troy) is a retired master sergeant and Andriea (aka Nete) is a nurse and was part of the Duke-Chapel Hill medical team. Bill had three children, ages eight, nine, and ten at the time and Nete had two children, ages ten and seventeen at the time. Bear in mind we already had three sons, ages three, six, and thirteen at the time. While taking all of these children in our household and caring for them was a daunting challenge, we grew closer as a family and became quite thrifty and organized. As I worked a full-time job as vice president and sales manager at First Union National Bank (now Wells Fargo), people would try to encourage my husband and me by saying "The Lord never puts more on you than you can bear." I remember one Sunday morning thinking, after getting up at 6:00 am to cook breakfast and get everybody ready for church, at Sunday School by 10:00 am, why God thought our shoulders were so big. Taking up an entire pew in church, we were on time and probably more organized than we are today. What a blessing was that incredible experience, giving all of us lifelong survival skills. All of the children have grown up to be beautiful adults and genuinely great people and contributors to society.

❧ **There's always a blue sky behind the darkest cloud.**

There's nothing more beautiful than a blue sky, beaming with a ray of hope. Even though being responsible for eight impressionable young people while their parents were serving our country was huge, we had some great times. Great people also came to our aid; family members, clients, and our church and bank families all played a vital role, even York Elementary PTSA where we had every grade covered. Church members brought food. Mrs. Sara Rochelle made the two girls, Ania and Katika, Easter dresses while Pastor Anita McMillan made sure that the children had special outings. Dion, Delante, Daryn, Ricky Jr. and Clayton strutted new suits for Easter from The Lion's Club shopping spree at Belks. Clients and bank associates took them to the circus, brought groceries, and showed many other acts of kindness. Wednesday was always "Bank Hump day" when one of my branches or departments came and brought food: a hot meal for the evening and enough milk, bread, and food to sustain us for the remainder of the week. These acts of kindness and love were refreshing rays of sunshine peeping through the clouds.

❧ **Why do you keep knocking your head against the brick wall?**

This was a message about stubbornness, denial, and disobedience. A brick wall doesn't move. If you hit it, the wall wins. When you were going around in circles, stubborn, in denial and didn't want to listen and heed sound instruction, this was expressed. In life, we knock our heads against brick walls when we insist on doing things our way. Some people have to experience brick wall moments for a crystal clear lesson.

❧ **The truth hurts.**

Hurting is painful. No matter how you try to justify or change things, the truth is the truth. When faced in a difficult situation, or developing a business strategy; stick to the facts. If you do, it minimizes emotions and opinions. The truth is sometimes painful. While it hurts, the truth is real and unchangeable. In many instances, we stay the size of a mustard seed until we accept and acknowledge the truth.

116

ᵧ **Your enemies will tell you your faults.**

Because your enemies have no agenda, they will tell you the painful truth about your faults. No matter who you are, even with the best intentions, you will have at least one enemy. It's just a part of life. Some enemies are the result of lack of communication and understanding. There is even value in having an enemy. It's an opportunity to engage in consensus building and dialogue. Your enemy has nothing to lose and will genuinely tell you your faults, faults that even people close to you wouldn't verbalize.

ᵧ **Let's put all the liars in the same room at the same time.**

"I didn't do it." These are the famous last words of any child. When there is lurking conflict, the best policy is to get all parties involved in the same room at the same time with discovery beginning and ending succinctly. Leadership takes strength, problem solving, and strong listening skills. Like sifting flour, you can get to the bottom of things and sift out the truth when forcing the players to play by the same rules. Your efforts in conflict resolution are a peace barometer for your team, household, church, or organization. This lesson on ownership and truth should be modeled through all hierarchies in our land.

ᵧ **There are two sides to every story.**

Conflict is inevitable. Communication and strong listening skills are necessary for resolve. As a parent, friend, pastor, counselor, sibling, or leader, refrain from taking sides until you've heard all sides. Before rushing to judgment, talk to both or all parties involved. Everyone has their side of the story and a justification for their perception. Great intervention comes when the two mutual sides merge with great compromise.

❧ **There are three sides to every story: his, hers, and the truth.**

Seeking the truth is a thing of beauty. When dissolving conflict after listening to all parties involved, the truth often lies somewhere in the middle. Ask multiple open-ended questions, keep an open mind, and vigorously seek the truth. This is more difficult when we try to disguise it or run away from it. Rest assured, it will eventually come out.

❧ **Just like churning makes butter, harsh words make fire.**

Growing up, homemade butter churned to perfection was a special treat. People would hand churn the curds, producing the sweetest tasting butter you've ever put in your mouth. This churned product was the perfect base of a scrumptious cake or topping for a mouth-watering homemade biscuit. As churning produces something powerful, harsh words produce fire. The tongue was often referred to as a fiery element, spreading gossip churning like fireballs. *A Chosen Seed* empowers, not destroys with fire.

❧ **Watch how you treat folks climbing up the ladder—they may have to catch you on the way down.**

Climbing up a ladder is relatively easy. Coming down takes care, skill, and patience to prevent a fall. In climbing the ladder of success, take caution in treating people fairly, with humility and compassion. If you snub people, they may be the same people that watch you as you fall back down. If they have any humility and compassion at all, they may be the ones who catch you or throw you the lifeline to safety. A similar version is, "Be careful how you treat people going up because you might pass them on the way down".

✦ **Be careful how you treat people because you never know who's going to give you your last drink of water.**

As a centurion, Granny has witnessed hundreds and thousands of births and deaths. Caring for people on their deathbed is a humbling and appointing experience. Being in a position of servant-hood, even to family members who have not always been kind to you, takes insurmountable and selfless strength. Not knowing what tomorrow may bring, this loud echo warns us to show love and compassion as we travel through life.

I see business leaders smile and move through this passively and not comprehend the intended leadership lesson and best practice. With the prevalent change in economic dynamics, with mergers, acquisitions, and human capital transitioning overnight, the implications are serious and life-threatening to business survival. Be very careful how you carry out your vision, mission, and employee satisfaction. The final drink of water corporately may well be an acquisition by an entity with which you had unscrupulous dealings. Former employees may be leading the new regime and you may end up on the bottom of the totem pole. Mergers and acquisitions are never equal. The final drink of water may be bitter with a lingering aftertaste.

❧ **Be careful how you treat people; you don't know whose behind you might have to kiss before you leave this world.**

Mrs. Jean Jones, whose beautiful mother is 102 years old, shared this from her family's memory. A spry warrior, Mrs. Clara Medlin is a trooper, armored with a smile for battles every day. As you get older and mature, you realize that the world gets smaller and smaller every day. This is an abundant reminder that the person that you mistreat may be the very person who has to do you a life-saving favor. No one knows what tomorrow might bring. Stay humble and treat others as you want to be treated.

❧ **You can't get to tomorrow by holding on to yesterday.**

Holding on to yesterday keeps you from letting go of the past. Absorb and learn from the lessons that yesterday provided, and build on these for a more promising today. Since life has no do-overs and you can't change what's already done, look forward to the beauty of tomorrow. Holding on to yesterday can stun you into numbness, immobilizing you to a withered seed.

❧ **Don't ever say what your children won't do. They will make you eat your words.**

To eat your words means you have to swallow your pride, saying something that obviously is not true. This was a compelling parenting and leadership lesson, of which I never fully comprehended the meaning until we had children and interfaced with teenagers and young, curious, and vibrant minds.

While this was spoken in the context of children, there's a valuable leadership lesson here. Be careful when you denounce what your children, team members, parishioners, or friends won't do. When positioned in a compromising situation, decision-making can be altered. Eating your own words can be too much dessert, putting your glucose level over the top. Depending on the severity, you may need an insulin injection.

❦ Everything in moderation.

Moderation is using self-control, temperance, and balance. Too much of any good thing can be taken to the extreme. Finding a balanced approach to any situation provides wholesome virtues. Prior to the financial crisis, moderation was an afterthought for most families. What began as frivolous spending habits resulted in a downward-spiraling society with record foreclosures, bankruptcies, and divorce rates. These record-breaking historical trends substantiate the need for everything in moderation.

❦ There's some good in everybody.

Since everyone has a purpose, there is good in even the worst criminal. You may just have to look a little harder to find it. As none of us are perfect, the lesson here is to focus on the good and positive attributes instead of dwelling on the imperfections. A pure spirit overrides a perfect spirit, as it appreciates the value in everybody. There's some good in every *Chosen Seed*.

❦ You're putting the cart before the horse.

Everyone knows that a horse can't pull anything unless he is in front, leading the way. When you prematurely jump to conclusions before assessing all the facts or when you begin a task before developing a strategy, then your execution is compromised with minimal results. All strategies in life have order. This was shared as a warning to always have a plan with all of your tools inside your cart, positioning yourself for a smooth ride.

ᶚ   I'm on the other side of through.

You can look into a person's eye and discern trouble. When people were having trials, lurking with troubled eyes, they would often say, "I'm going through." When they came out of their wilderness experience with an answered prayer, their response was, "I'm on the other side of through." In other words, *through* is the tribulation and *the other side* represents the answered prayer, relief, and day of hope, sunshine, and joy. With various stages and periods, trials are made to strengthen us. The length of your trial is paralleled with grasping the lesson(s) being taught as you venture to *the other side* of through.

ᶚ   Letting the cat out of the bag is a whole lot easier than putting it back in.

Chosen seeds are gifted containers. They contain and maintain many secrets and confidences, while others can't wait to share someone else's news. Once you let others' confidential issues out, i.e. the cat out of the bag, it's impossible to retract it. When someone honors you with their trust, hold it dear to your heart and cherish it. Silence is golden.

❧ **The man with no shoes felt sorry for himself until he met a man with no feet.**

One of the most beautiful attributes that Granny possesses and passed as a legacy to her children is a high tolerance for pain, both emotional and physical. Even when you were in severe pain, she would say, "Just grin and bear it." We were always appreciative of even the smallest gifts. We had compassion for others and those less fortunate. Bear in mind, we didn't have money, but our wealth was evident by love, and the necessities of food and shelter. Material possessions were unimportant as long as you had a happy heart filled with strong core values. To make this plain and relevant to today's economy, "The man/woman who complained of a bad job felt sorry for himself until he met many men/women with no job."

❧ **When you find yourself in a hole, stop digging.**

To dig a hole takes hard work and constant effort. This is a hard lesson on introspection because we are the source of our own problems. If you constantly find yourself in a hole, stop and breathe. Take the time to meditate and honestly assess the situation. When you give yourself permission to slow down and be brutally honest, you can trace back to the root of the problem.

If you have an infection, you can't just treat it with topical creams or other remedies. The infection may be in your bloodstream, thus internal treatment is necessary. Only an antibiotic will keep the infection from spreading, healing you from the inside out. Treating it only from the exterior has certainty of a reoccurrence, perhaps a fatal one.

When you're in a hole, an honest assessment may prohibit a reoccurrence.

> **The biggest troublemaker in your life is staring you in the mirror.**

A mirror is unforgiving. What you see is what you get. This lesson warns you of self-defeating tactics. We are our own worst enemies. Self-defeating talk, allowing yourself to fall into depression, and living in the past are great challenges that keep you from moving forward and bearing great fruit. Passionately moving forward, look into the mirror and encourage yourself.

> **Wallow with pigs and you'll surely get dirty.**

Pigs are dirty and smelly but everyone loves them when they're on your table. Wallowing with pigs means you're associating with the wrong crowd or making bad decisions. When you make a conscious decision to associate or have dealings with persons who are unlikely to change, then your results will maintain the same. Over time, no amount of soap or borax will clean up the dirt.

> **Two wrongs don't make a right.**

If you make one bad decision and are suffering the consequences, it's easy to make a secondary bad decision. At some point you have to determine how high of a price you're willing to pay. While it's difficult to stop and get on the right track, begin today with turning the situation around because not only do two wrongs not make a right, they make matters worse.

❦ **This too shall pass.**

We considered the passing of time as the healing of all hurts. Heartaches are inevitable but, in time, the pain lessens. It may never go away completely but the depth and the severity of pain will ease up. Yolanda Adams has a befitting song titled, "This Too Shall Pass." Its lyrics are a lesson in themselves:

> In the middle of the turbulence surrounding you
> These trying times that are so hard to endure
> In the middle of what seems to be your darkest hour
> Hold fast your heart and be assured.
>
> This too shall pass
> Like every night that's come before it
> He'll never give you more than you can bear
> This too shall pass
> So in this thought be comforted
> It's in His hands
> This too shall pass.

CHAPTER 7

Abundance

• • •

Abundance occurs at full maturity after completing a long sought-after goal or dream. Abundance is everlasting. Seeds, plants, and trees that grow in abundance have a legacy, returning year after year with continuous growth and vibrancy. *Chosen Seeds* are intended to be life–fulfilling, their legacy felt for generations to come. When a seed comes to full maturity, the beauty is amazingly breathtaking.

When we plant seeds, we never know which one will prosper and be that *Chosen Seed*. What is intended to prosper will prosper at the perfect time. Continuing to sow seeds will bring fruit and an abundant harvest; seeds of love, seeds of integrity, and seeds of selflessness. While we didn't grow up with money or lots of material possessions, our wealth is in the lessons learned. Granny's most impactful lessons are love, instilling an incredibly strong work ethic, integrity tested over time, and the value of selflessness. These *Grannyisms*™ prove that manifestations of abundance shall prevail in due season.

Honor is given to Granny's siblings, *Chosen Seeds* who side-by-side weathered the storms of life. Laura Shaw, Armetro Cole and Ernestine Cromartie are living testimonies of abundance that began as a mustard seed. The legacies of deceased siblings Wade Shaw, Taft Shaw, Wiley Shaw Jr., Cora Shaw, Helen Jones, Ruby Shaw and Ruth Riddick continue to blaze paths from foundational seeds already laid.

Abundant Living

· · · ·

℣ **The Lord is my shepherd, I shall not want.**

This is one of Granny's favorites; at one hundred years old, she can still recite almost the entire Twenty-third Psalm, as it is engrained in her spirit. While she was sitting on our couch one day, between nodding and talking about the earlier years, she'd say, "Lord remember me. The Lord is my shepherd." While I've heard this passage all of my life, I marveled that day, thinking about what "my Shepherd" to a centurion might really mean. The imagery is beautiful: totally depending and trusting in God to take care of her every need. Because the saying is true that you're "once an adult and twice a child"; when you're one hundred years old, you are dependent on someone for everything. There's abundance for *A Chosen Seed* to know that the "Shepherd" will take care of all your needs. As she has been in His flock, the Shepherd has protected her through poverty, not having a right to vote, not having the best mechanism for education, sitting on the back of the bus, walking everywhere she went, living through pure hatred, physical and mental abuse, and being berated as a woman with nine children with just enough scraps to make ho-cake bread (meal, water, and salt mixture) to feed her children.

To live long enough to witness President Barack Obama inaugurated as president of the United States and Governor Beverly Purdue as the first woman governor in North Carolina is breathtaking. To witness her grandchildren and great-grandchildren graduate year after year from colleges, exceeding and making their indelible mark in the business, technology, sales, engineering, medical, sports industries and many others is an awe-filled historical time. Having walked through the valley of the shadow of death, to be coherent and in her right mind is a true and almost inconceivable gift for this sheep. He has restored her through so many tumultuous turns. For one hundred years, grace, goodness, and mercy have followed and without a shadow of a doubt, a table has already been prepared for her to dwell in HIS house forever.

As a shepherd of people in your employ, what are the ways that demonstrate your actions to do everything in your power to protect and ensure their well-being? What are the ways that your flock genuinely puts their trust in you? Give examples of how you have provided for their physical, mental, and spiritual needs. What shows that they'd like to dwell in your place of business or even be connected to it in the future?

ﭪ   **Be careful how you live. You might be the only BIBLE a lot of people read.**

In Granny's era, life is synonymous with a story line. While she is an avid reader still today, many in her day couldn't read; lessons were instead taught by life's experiences. The BIBLE was our golden book. Its sixty-six chapters created a road map, a lamp for our paths to follow, and the proper light for navigation. Just as many of the *Grannyisms*™ were passed down to her from her parents, the life we lived was in essence the Bible that people saw. Instructions were taught in the character and integrity of handling day-to-day occurrences. It was more important that you lived a life of careful walking because you and your life would be the only Bible that many would ever read.

❧ Lord (pronounced LAWD by Granny) remember me.

Growing up, we always heard Granny humming and singing as she cooked, quilted, did laundry, and went about her merry way. Humming often masked the pain she felt and singing was a reminder of better days ahead. An old spiritual, "Lord Remember Me" was a plea for God to look over her and provide for the family. At one hundred years old, she moans constantly, "Lawd, remember me." "Amazing Grace" and "Walk with Me Lord" are her other favorite hymns. If you're on the phone talking with someone and she is in another part of the house where she can't see you, she'll strike out in one of her hymns. This is her way of getting you to come and sit in front of her where she can see you. While she can't recall many things, she seems to remember what's important. We all know that the constant praying and asking for blessings over her children and family is a huge contributor to our success today. We are all blessed and living on her prayers.

❧ Count it all joy.

One can look at their situation and allow themselves to be depressed. Whether you have peace, joy, or are full of depression, it is a choice. It is a choice of your attitude and state of mind. Only you can choose to make a transformation. The beauty about being surrounded by a community who grew up tough and poor by today's standards is that you always found something for which to be thankful. You ultimately counted it all joy—unspeakable joy. When you learn to experience joy, your blessings become abundant. The hard economic times today are bearable because we know what hard times are, because we've lived them. We used coupons and pinched pennies when it wasn't popular and cool. We count it all joy because every penny has ALWAYS had a purpose, not just today when pennies are few for all. "Count it all joy when you fall into various trials, knowing that the testing of your faith produces patience." (James 1:2-3)

> **God loves a cheerful giver.**

A cheerful giver gives unselfishly and with joy! Giving and not looking for anything in return. There is a difference in being a giver and being a *cheerful* giver. When you give cheerfully, you give from the heart, not desiring of any public display and most often in silence. A cheerful giver doesn't begrudge their deeds, and will give bountifully without being asked. When they feel in their heart to give of their time, energy, and financial resources, they give with love and joy. There's a startling fact about cheerful givers: they are ALWAYS blessed, even in the midst of a storm. I am so thankful because I grew up with not just a family of givers, but a community of *cheerful* givers. All of the cheerful givers were our Mamas because they would give you a cheerful whooping if you needed it as well. I realize that whooping is not proper English, but I am confirming that we received *whoopings* and not *whippings* or *spankings*. Wonderful Mamas like Mrs. Mamie Spaulding, Mrs. Gladys Moore, Mrs. Agnes Lennon, Mrs. Celia Little, Mrs. Lula Graham, Mrs. Katie Johnson, Mrs. Pearlie Rouse,

Mrs. Elizabeth Laws, Mrs. Alzenia Lennon and Mrs. Betty Johnson. While some of them are deceased, their giving spirit remains. Amazingly, their legacies are also cheerful givers. If I traveled home to Whiteville, NC today and needed anything, I could call the children or grandchildren of any of these women and they would come to my aid. The fruit from these *Chosen Seeds* are still blessing others.

The biblical reference is very direct in 2 Corinthians 9:6-7: "But this I say: he who sows sparingly will also reap sparingly, and he who sows bountifully will also reap bountifully. So let each one give as he purposes in his heart, not grudgingly or of necessity; for God loves a cheerful giver."

❧ **Stay prayed up.**

The older ladies, especially Mama Agnes Lennon, my class leader, would tell you to "stay prayed up," particularly when you came home to visit after going away to college, etc. We religiously had to learn Bible verses and recite them. They would tell you that it's okay for someone else to pray for you but you needed to know how to pray for yourself and at some point you'd be in a predicament or sick and you needed to know how to get a voice up to heaven or call the Lord yourself.

❧ **The Lord takes care of babies and fools.**

I used to laugh when Granny said this, only to live five decades and realize that with some of the decisions I've made, He's still taking care of me, and I'm certainly not a baby. What about you?

֍   **All things work together for good.**

Working to achieve a common goal, a family or team pulls together to fulfill a greater purpose. Even in bad times, Granny knew that all things worked together for the purpose intended. As a matter of fact, Romans 8:28 says: "We know that all things work together for good for those who love God, and are called according to his purpose."

֍   **I can do all things through Christ who strengthens me.**

It takes strength and determination to reach any goal. This is actually one of her favorite passages, as well as one of mine. At Granny's centennial celebration, our son Clayton shared this favorite scriptural reference. A strong, determined, and feisty lady with limited resources, she was convinced that she could do just about anything she positioned her mind to achieve. Philippians 4:13 is the source for her century-aged determination and goal-oriented nature. She is still convinced that she can take care of herself, live alone in her own house, cook biscuits, and prepare meals, as she did in her youth. She doesn't give up easily, even if you tell her repeatedly otherwise.

That determined strength is what keeps her going. She received a congratulatory letter and picture from President Obama that was framed in a gorgeous plaque for her birthday. Determined that she could do all things through Christ who strengthens, she informed us recently that she was leaving, going home and taking President Obama with her. Let's see how that's going to work for her.

☙ **Seven days without God makes you weak.**

On the farm, if you were too weak to work, or anytime you felt sick, there was a home remedy to bring you back to life: wormwood tea, sassafras tea, or castor oil would miraculously strengthen your health. No matter what was going on, after a week you would be in church on Sunday. You could go out Saturday night and be sleepy on Sunday if you chose but you were absolutely going to be in church on Sunday morning. In the early days, you were in church all day long, from Sunday School to worship service and then to some kind of afternoon program. As a matter of fact, none of us can remember missing a Sunday even through sickness, rain, sleet, snow, or exhausting heat. Sunday was non-negotiable as we spent Saturday preparing for Sunday's dinner. From laundry on washboards to wringing the chicken's neck in the backyard, cleaning it in hot scalding water, plucking the feathers, and syringing them for further preparation. The chicken was then soaked in salt and vinegar water, parboiled, seasoned, and was then ready to make a million chicken delicacies. Yes, this was hard work for one chicken but it was necessary to ensure cleanliness and a tasty Sunday meal. The chicken was so clean that the FDA would have to revise their standards. Potatoes would be peeled, vegetables picked, shelled, cleaned, and ready for the pot. The cakes, pies, or cobblers were made from scratch and perfectly displayed overnight awaiting the first morsel. I know some people are shaking their heads in disbelief to the amount of work involved. Hard work was the norm, the way of life not just for our family but everyone. Don't knock it. Other than a fluid pill, Granny takes no medication and wears no glasses while each of her children do both. I'm sure that in one hundred years, she has never gone seven days without God. That's why she is healthy as a horse.

☙   **The Lord will make a way somehow.**

With nine children to raise and limited financial means, this was a source of encouragement and hope for tomorrow. Granny was not a great singer but loved to sing and hum old hymns while cooking. Humming and cooking went hand in hand, like poetry in motion. We believers all know that the economy may seem bleak but the Lord will make a way somehow. This is also a spiritual written by Thomas Dorsey:

"The Lord Will Make A Way Somehow"

Like a ship that's tossed and driven, battered by an angry sea;
when the storms of life are raging, and their fury falls on me.
I wonder what I have done, that makes this race so hard to run;
then I say to my soul, take courage, the Lord will make a way somehow.

The Lord will make a way somehow, when beneath the cross I bow,
He will take away each sorrow; let Him have your burdens now.
When the loads bears down so heavy the weight is shown upon my brow,
there's a sweet relief in knowing the Lord will make a way somehow.

⚡   **He'll make a way out of no way.**

This may be receiving unexpected money in the nick of time to pay the light bill or making a complete meal with one chicken breast. That one chicken breast was carefully proportioned, sliced and diced into a huge casserole or smothered in a big pot with dumplings and chicken parts of giblets, necks, backs, and feet over hot, steamy rice. Yes, we really ate the giblets, necks, backs, and chicken feet as a meal and were mighty grateful. This *Grannyism*™ gave her hope out of what was seemingly a hopeless situation. In our businesses and personal lives, there is always a miraculous occurrence that comes out of nowhere just in the nick of time, making a way out of no way.

⚡   **Words like deeds bear fruit.**

You can't un-say unkind words. The power of our words can be everlasting, pushing others forward or creating a cement hole. How many of us remember something that was said to us at a very early age, even five or six? These words, like our deeds, either harvest into fruit, producing a crop to feed a multitude, or diminish our dreams. Many dreams are destroyed and unfulfilled because of words imparted as a child.

In business, words and deeds drive revenue. Profitability is driven by consistent and genuine fruit.

⚡   **Riches ain't measured by money.**

Money is in no way evil but a deep love of money is the root of evil. A rich spirit filled with integrity, character, and a genuine heart has more value than one who simply possesses dollars. Dollars and no sense is a dangerous combination in the corporate world and at home.

❧ Be the salt that you are.

Salt is intended to be a seasoning agent. Too much salt makes a meal un-enjoyable and can cause major health complications. Not having enough salt in your diet can also cause hardship, therefore maintaining a healthy balance is necessary. Such is life. Our business and personal lives are intended to provide seasonings to make our surroundings a better place, providing worthy service to our communities.

❧ Tasteless salt is worthless.

Why have salt if it's tasteless? Apply this to your multiple roles. If we are all salt, the sprinkles that are seen and felt should have meaning, value, and worth. If you are not making a significant contribution, the time is ripe to reevaluate. If you're in a marriage, employment, or other circumstance and feel as though your value index has been compromised, then your tasty season is probably over.

❧ Let your little light shine.

Your light is the reflection of your character and daily actions. Your daily walk is to provide a pathway illuminated by your service and edifying others. Granny always did things sincerely, never taking credit while providing light through a seemingly dark path. Regardless of your focus, mission, or vision, this example should be included in your strategic execution so that your little light becomes a beacon.

❧ The best thing you'll ever have is your reputation.

Your family name was perceived to be worth gold, and your reputation was considered worth pure gold. Whatever mistakes you made, you were always reminded that both the family name and your reputation could be tarnished. Whether the perception was real or not, it was perceived to be real. A business reputation is all you have, perceptions real or unreal.

❧ A candle don't lose nothing by lighting another one.

As a candle, you can light the candles of others over and over; bringing light into hundreds and thousands of lives. The beauty of lighting the candle of others is that your light will keep burning with the impact getting brighter and brighter, never dimmer. It loses nothing by sharing, but advances its value by being used as a light source for others. I'm amazed by people who withhold information when teaching and coaching, especially with employees. They'd rather keep the knowledge than spice up someone else's life. I have sadly witnessed bankers and sales leaders purposely not impart knowledge and wisdom to others, even their direct reports. Their sad mindset of "I'm not teaching him/her, because they might outshine me" attitude is selfish and demeaning because they have everything to gain and nothing to lose by lighting the candle of another. To witness this in religious settings is even sadder. Pushing others up by lighting their candle is a selfless gift that screams of getting back to the basic principles of living. Abundance comes by sharing your lighted candle. Not passing your light on is the same as having an unlit candle and tasteless salt of worthless value.

❧ **If you want your dreams to come true, then wake up.**

Waking up from a vivid dream can give one motivation. Dreams do come true, but only with strategic planning, a focused mind, and concise execution. The answer to our dream is sometimes right in front of our eyes. Being too close in a situation sometimes skews your vision, blocking the real perspective. When this happens, taking a quiet moment and reassessing will lead to a clearer vision.

❧ **All things are possible if you only believe.**

Believing is a powerful fundamental. People who believe in themselves are more successful. Having the right mindset is half of the battle to winning. The person who thinks they can win will.

❧ **Figure out early if the glass is half full or half empty.**

If you're thirsty and have two glasses of water, one half full and one half empty, they both have the exact same amount of thirst-quenching liquid. It's all a matter of your attitude and mindset whether you perceive it as being half full or half empty. This semantic enables you to navigate life with a different level of perspective. Your attitude absolutely does determine your altitude.

As a business, is your corporate vision being executed as half full or half empty? Personally, is your life path being executed as half full or half empty? The answers rest with your attitude and mindset.

⚡ It's better to limp all the way to heaven than not to get there at all.

Limping parlays a struggle and heaven can be applied to any goal for which you strived. Every life and every business has struggles. Trials and stresses are inevitable but if you decide to stop too soon, you'll never claim your rewards. Your ranking in life is unimportant once you're in. Once you reach your goals, how you got there or your ranking becomes unimportant.

⚡ Give credit where credit is due.

Truly unselfish leaders are appreciative of their core team and are gifted to share the spotlight, giving credit to the right persons for their contributions, diligence, and hard work. Managers and other self-absorbed persons in positional power enjoy taking all of the credit for the core success. While their motives are self-serving, they miss the big picture and rob the company of future profits. Confident leaders are the first ones to give credit where credit is due and will be the first to be accountable when problems arise. As stated earlier, doing the right thing is a foundation for building long-lasting relationships versus simply performing transactions. "Do not withhold good from those to whom it is due, when it is in the power of your hand to do so." Proverbs 3:27

⚡ Good judgment comes from experience. Experience comes from bad judgment.

Life's swift transitions provide the experiences for which we use the learned lessons to pave lighter pathways. Some of our experiences result from the consequences of our decisions, bad judgment, risk taking, or simply not knowing. Grasping the lessons will fuel wiser future decisions, overshadowing both ignorance and naiveté.

⚹ **Don't put all your eggs in one basket.**

When going to the chicken coop to gather eggs, you usually had a sturdy basket in which to store them. If the hens and chickens laid both white and brown eggs, you would take two baskets for separation. Eggs refer to your blessings, usually those of money, finances, or some kind of investment. This adage encouraged you to diversify and have a backup plan. Having lived through the Depression, Granny's wisdom overshadowed Wall Street with the many bank failures that occurred in the two years before this writing. Many who lost their entire retirement savings during the recent recession could have utilized this advice, giving us another indication that wisdom dominates over education and pedigrees.

⚹ **Keep several irons in the fire.**

We had several long, black iron pokers to stir up the fire in the burning wood stove and heater. Navigating life takes diversifying your plans, modifying your thoughts, constantly upgrading your skills, and keeping several irons in the fire. This is very similar to the "don't put all of your eggs in one basket" theory. Keeping at least two or three revenue streams provides continuous heat and ensures a constant burning flame.

⚹ **Different strokes for different folks.**

Our differences are our strengths. We're more alike than we are different. It's the appreciation of our diversity that provides propelling heights. Two of us will arrive at the same conclusion but our thought processes may get us there by a different direction. The importance is that we reach the same conclusion. Even when we don't get to the same conclusion, learning and appreciating one another's different thoughts and opinions is healthy. Life would be ever so dull if we were all robots.

❧ **Count your blessings; name them one by one.**

As I was sitting at the Cancer Center of North Carolina for blood work, as a result of a blood clot, this saying came to mind. It is also an old Negro spiritual:

> Count your blessings, name them one by one.
> Count your blessings, see what God has done.

Being at the Cancer Center with people in all stages of cancer gave me a new appreciation for life. There were many patients who would have traded their cancer for my blood clot in a heartbeat, as every minute, every hour of every day is more precious than gold. Wow, how this can be applied to every arena of your life. Even in business, if you're having struggles—at least you have a job, providing revenue for your family, so be thankful. If you have pains, at least you can feel the pain. There are many who would trade places with you. This is a fabulous exercise if you're having a pity party or a distressed moment. Count your blessings. Name them one by one. It changes your perspective.

❧ **When praises go up, blessings come down.**

This is scriptural; Matthew 21:22. Despite life's circumstances, when you're thankful and give praise for the everyday things, blessings seem to come down and abundantly shower your family, your business, and every seed that you touch. Obedience is the elementary stage of ultimate blessings. When you obey those in authority, the sweet fruit reaped from obedience seeds are unexplainable. Deuteronomy 28:3-4, 6 exclaims, "Blessed shall you be in the city, and blessed shall you be in the country. Blessed shall be the fruit of your body, the produce of your ground and the increase of your herds, the increase of your cattle and the offspring of your flocks. Blessed shall you be, when you come in, and blessed shall you be when you go out." When praises go up, blessings do come down.

⚘ Praise Him from whom all blessings flow.

This was actually the doxology in the AME Zion church growing up. As a little girl, I was puzzled as to why older folks would just quote this out of context for seemingly no reason at all. Granny had nine children of her own and had a hand in raising her grandchildren as well. Now I realize, just to be able to feed a hot meal to all these little hungry people was a reason to give Praise for no reason.

A doxology is a short hymn that's sung as part of a worship service. The actual lyrics and biblical origin are:

> Praise God from Whom all blessings flow.
> Praise Him, all creatures here below;
> Praise Him above, ye heavenly Hosts.
> Praise Father, Son and Holy Ghost".

"Every good gift and perfect gift is from…the Father," James 1:17, provides affirmation that we need to praise Him from whom all blessings flow.

❧ **A good name is worth more than silver and gold.**

Growing up in our family, neighborhood, church, and school, a good name was all that you had. Since no one had any money, a good name was priceless and it was imperative that you didn't do anything to tarnish your name because it not only affected you, but your entire family and community. Boy, do we need this lesson today. People really took pride in preserving their largest asset, "the family name." Somewhere along the line of climbing to the top, we left this precious jewel on the bottom rung and forgot to bring it with us. The biblical references are powerful: Proverbs 22:1, "A good name is to be chosen rather than great riches, Loving favor rather than silver and gold"; Ecclesiastes 7:1a, "A good name is better than precious ointment."

A good name was equated to your character and reputation. If you polled your family, colleagues, business associates, and your clients and asked them to anonymously provide the first word that comes to mind when describing:

❧ Your individual name

❧ Your business name

What would the results be? Could you publish them?

❧ **To whom much is given, much is expected.**

It was just expected of our family to be servants and givers, with unselfish motives. It was an inherent and instinctive part of who we were. We didn't have much but you could always look around and see someone else who was worse

145

off than we were. This speaks to all walks of your life and especially in business. There are so many philanthropic causes and multiple community needs to fill. To create purposeful giving, choose a passion that feeds your spirit. Luke 12:48b exclaims, "For everyone to whom much is given, from whom much will be required." This requirement of service and giving bring a lifetime of abundance.

- **Hard work beats talent when talent don't beat hard work.**

Some people are gifted and blessed with natural and extraordinary abilities to excel. Even with incredible gifted-ness, it takes a matching amount of hard work and perspiration to bring the talents to their ultimate, prized status. All professional athletes have to work hard for their talents to be exhibited and so do corporate leaders. If you're on a sales or athletic team or playing in the game of life, having an esteemed work ethic and putting in 110 percent of consistent effort will almost always overshadow the more talented but slothful competitor.

- **When you forgive your enemies, it messes up their head.**

Forgiveness is hard, but with a pure heart, you can do it more easily. Forgiving others releases you, freeing you to explore life and celebrate its gifts. Forgiving is more about you than the other person, as not forgiving builds a poison that spreads all over your body. When you forgive and forget, the offender is astonished because they'd love for you to remain in captivity. To the offender, forgiving them and going about your daily walk is confusing, baffling, and really messes up their head. Try it. Leave them astonished and live in abundance.

Ain't nothing new under the sun.

This means there will be a repeat of past history. History has a way of repeating itself over and over again. Fades, wars, rumors of wars, famine, hurt, fear, pain, murder, and children against parents are all a repeat of history. Be assured that when you choose, you can endure and overcome obstacles. There's comfort in knowing that someone or some business has been a pioneer and has tackled and surpassed all the challenges that you are facing. A solid foundation allows you to rise to the top, maybe bruised and scorned, but with resilience.

Ecclesiastes 1:9 says: "That which has been is what will be. That which is done is what will be done. And there is nothing new under the sun."

A penny wise and a pound foolish.

Being wise in your spending is a prudent practice. When we set out to begin a project, if we don't carefully count up the cost at the onset, it generally causes us to spend twice the amount of money overall. Instead of hiring legal counsel or spending a few dollars for wise strategic prevention measures upfront, we set out on our exploration, ill advised. Once trouble arises, we then seek assistance costing more time, money, and energy for a resolution. This piece of wisdom is relative to "an ounce of prevention is worth a pound of cure" and will bring much abundance in your life.

Biblically, we are instructed to prioritize and sort out the opportunities before us (Psalm 32:8), and proceed in an effective and timely manner. List the tasks and goals at hand, consider the timetable (Colossians 2:5), and arrange them in order of priority (1Corinthinans 14:40).

If it involves financial resources, count up all of your cost, leaving a cushion for life's un-expectancies. This is a sad reminder of many churches who embark on a construction project only to get 50 to 75 percent complete with no more funds. Luke 14:28-30 has a harsh warning: "for which of you, intending to build a tower does not sit down first and count the cost, whether he has enough to finish it. Lest, after he has laid the foundation, and is not able to finish, all who see it begin to mock him saying, this man began to build and was not able to finish." Now that's a penny wise and a pound foolish.

⚡ **God works in mysterious ways.**

Granny would tell all of us this, not knowing exactly the depth of the meaning. As life's experiences mold you, you realize the power of this message. It's almost majestic as you reflect on the past. Life is a mystery and the lessons revealed show His omnipotent power.

While I had several manuscripts that had already been completed, breaking my ankle gave me the opportunity to pray, reflect, read, and listen while enjoying porch tranquility. In my meditation, this book was written, predominantly by dreams. The dreams were so real that I began to record the times and everything that I could remember. The journaling is a masterpiece all in itself, revelations of personal and corporate encounters. Promises of restorations and overflowing blessings are mapped out more perfectly than any business strategy I have developed for a client. The predominance of being awakened at 3:33 am has special meaning, from the number of *Grannyisms*™ printed to the direction of the Trinity to the strategic road map already laid out, soaring to heal nationally and internationally. The fruit produced from *A Chosen Seed* will heal many hearts and provide an ordained platform for integrity and ethical best business practices to inspire centuries to come.

Yes Granny, God does work in mysterious ways!

⚡ He didn't bring me this far to leave me.

This is a lesson in perseverance: keep moving forward even when you don't think you can lift another muscle. This is an insurance policy and a solution for despair, hopelessness, joblessness, and the perils of life. If you can just reflect on your personal and business life: you didn't get where you are by standing still. Granny was determined that her family have an abundant life both here on earth and beyond. What she and others lacked in education, she overpowered with wisdom. This is the true difference in *knowledge* and *wisdom*. Having knowledge is knowing that you need to put one foot ahead of the other and continuously move forward. Wisdom reflects on the journey, guiding you to appreciate every past hurt or danger during the quest. Wisdom quenches your thirst for more, knowing that the cooling satisfaction will come when you reach your pinnacle, even with a spirit of genuine and sincere gratitude for the people who purposely stuck their foot in your path for you to fall or dug a hole for your demise. Wisdom is having discernment and miraculously being given a keen vision of the placement of shovel and dirt, and a detoured road to travel.

Even with all odds against you, assure yourself that as *A Chosen Seed*, HE didn't bring you this far to leave you. In order to win the race, you have to stay in it. Keep moving forward, striding one step at a time. If HE brought you this far, HE's still carrying you. Enjoy the ride!

⚡ Do what you can live with!

One of my best friends from Winston-Salem State University, and a lifetime prayer warrior, Sandra Stewart Farrow, would say this all of the time. Her mom, Mrs. Mettie Stewart, is the origin of this powerful *Grannyism*™. When you think about it, this should be posted in every home and office across the globe—maybe throughout the jails and prisons. Taking us back to the basics, its deep and simple meaning is so parallel to the Golden Rule.

Do what you can live with! Each day of our lives, we're faced with decisions and the resulting consequences. With lingering effects, decisions of:

- Treating people fairly vs. having deliberate inequalities
- Displaying honesty over double tongues of deception
- Planting bountiful seeds instead of destroying kernels
- Serving with kindness and empathy without insincerity and stinging harshness

- Sowing with compelling potency instead of sparse sprinklings
- Speaking life from the power of your tongue in lieu of spewing poisonous venom
- Showing gratitude instead of entitlement
- Controlling one's self and not manipulating interactions
- Exhibiting benevolence and visionary spending with every penny fulfilling a purpose vs. frivolous and greed
- Loving unconditionally and not just when it's convenient

When you do what you can live with, life's rewards grant us FAVOR. This favor is a priceless jewel, misunderstood and baffling to many. FAVOR mystifies, elevates, and blesses you out of nowhere, fitting you with skates to maneuver around the well-planned pitfalls intended for your fall.

While people in high places and wealthy resources can buy tons of material possessions, I get joy in assurance that FAVOR can't be purchased or bought with any amount of money, for with FAVOR you are the beneficiary of the greatest Estate ever imagined.

Do what you can live with! "Now to Him who is able to do exceedingly abundantly above all that we ask or think, according to the power that works in us, to Him be glory to all generations forever and ever. AMEN." Ephesians 3:20-21.

❧ **Don't be so heavenly bound that you're no earthly good.**

We all have people in our path that are so "spirit filled" but not necessarily "full of the spirit." While none of us should judge, let's stick to the facts.

- Do you know individuals who are so holy that they don't get along with anyone?
- Do you know individuals who can quote many verses of scripture but their walk doesn't match the talk?
- Do you know individuals who preach benevolence but rarely lend a helping hand?
- Do you know individuals who shout and stamp religiously but use those same feet to run away from the commitment of serving?
- Do you know individuals who would rather pray for the hungry than prepare a meal for them?

Some of you are ready to turn the page without finishing reading this because you think it doesn't apply to you. Well, if you are an individual, I guarantee that you have someone in your circle or family who fits the bill. If you're in business or work outside of the home, I guarantee this person is on your staff or in your organization, infiltrating themselves around like an exterminator.

These attributes are what Granny and other wise elders meant that match these descriptions of being heavenly bound but no earthly good, grappling with fake deception and selfishness. Contemplate on how one by one, we could elevate abundance in our families, communities, states, and countries around the globe by eradicating this one attribute.

☞ **Your setback is gonna wind up being a miracle.**

Have you ever had the worst happen to you at the absolute worst time? Lost a job, a loved one, your biggest client, a profitable sale that fell apart, had an accident while you were on total commission, been in the midst of downsizing, reengineering, or any of the new human resource terms we have for "no income"? Divorce, separation, or any of life's throwbacks that leave you flat on your back? Don't fret; it may end up being your biggest blessing. I've heard older people and ministers say all my life that life's pain or setbacks could end up being your greatest miracles. Many successful and profitable businesses result out of someone losing their job.

After being out of work and running the daily operations of our companies for nine months, I know without a shadow of a doubt that breaking my ankle and ending up with a blood clot was ordained. No, I'm not crazy; I recognize that this was part of God's plan for my life in this particular season. It was ordained that my primary care physician sent me to a hematologist practicing at a cancer center. I leave after each visit having a greater appreciation for life each day. The patients at the cancer center are all so special as they endure an extremely tough blow in their life.

Through this interaction, many of them have a gift of prophecy to share with me:

- "You get to fire your hematologist; most of us won't"
- "There's a lot of folks here who'd trade you for your blood clot"

- "You must have something great coming your way to be off your feet for such a long time"
- "He's giving you plenty of rest for what's in store"
- "Your setback ain't nothing but a setup for a comeback" (Version from Joel Osteen quote)

While I'm not thrilled or happy about the pain associated with this process, I'm truly blessed knowing that there will be more gain that comes out of this ordeal than pain. As the orthopedic surgeon indicated when I tore my ankle up, I am indeed an example of perseverance even in the midst of adversity. I would hear Granny's voice in my mind saying, "Grin and bear it." One of the most important blessings is an attitude of gratitude and to not ask, "Why did God allow this to happen," but emphatically acclaim that *"this is a mighty God who will sustain me in all the things HE allows to happen."*

Because God uses simple and ordinary people to accomplish HIS great purposes, this setback in my personal and business life was not only a miracle but a setup for a miraculous comeback, for I, too, like Granny, am *A CHOSEN SEED*.

⚡ **I don't know what the future holds, but I know who holds the future.**

These reflections from the past will save our future if we put our trust in the One who holds the future. Having a broken ankle that required a permanent steel plate, seven pins, and blood clots that baffled the doctors and radiologists, was a time of reflection, prioritizing, and giving me a new perspective on life. Rowing each day in unchartered waters gave me a refreshed spirit and new appreciation.

Rocking my pain away on the porch one morning, His voice whispered, "I have raised you up for this very purpose of displaying MY power in you, so that MY name may be proclaimed the whole world over." (Romans 9:17)

"Eye has not seen, nor ear heard, nor have entered into the heart of man the things which God has prepared for those who love HIM." (I Corinthians 2:9) Step into your destiny with the One who holds the future.

ᘓ **Cherish your front row.**

In each of our lives, we have people, including clients, relationship partners, family, and friends in our front row. A person who is valuable enough to have a seat on your front row, edifies, builds up, and sustains your spirit. Front-row participants share your emotions, dreams, and pain, being there when you're happy or sad. In business, front-row participants are mutually beneficial, providing a win-win.

Some front-row participants come in and out of our personal and professional lives during trials, storms, and seasons. The beauty of a front-row influencer is that you may not see them daily but their prayers can be felt and can reach you at the most opportune time. Along with significant others, I'm blessed to have college friends on my front row. We entered Winston Salem State University in 1976 scared out of our minds but today we are accomplished in our own fields. Who knew that we would be *Chosen Seeds* to have a lasting bond thirty years later with a seeded purpose? While distant, my collegiate front row has proven that prayer moves like a super highway.

While everyone can't be in your front row, don't count your balcony out. People in the balcony have the potential to be front-row participants but during this particular season, more cultivation is needed. With the right soil, nourishment, and timing, they may become front-runners for a front-row seat.

Always cherish your front row by handling them with care, showing them love and appreciation. As life would have it, some folks may need to be kept in the balcony. Folks without substance need to be kept outside. Those seemingly on a treadmill going nowhere don't need to be kept at all. Wisdom will help you determine the right positioning for the right time.

⚯ **Cream always rises to the top.**

Our next-door neighbor growing up made homemade butter. Mrs. Mamie Spaulding, now deceased, had an intense, methodical, step-by-step process that yielded perfection. The perfectly round, finished pound of butter was light, sweet, and one of the most pure and savory tastes that ever touched my taste buds. To say that it was scrumptious is an understatement and just the starting point. The love of her craft and the joy that it brought to her face elevated the taste. The Spauldings raised their own cows, which was the genesis of the process. These cows grazing in the sprawling, green country pastures of greens, fruits, and vegetables produced the most delicious, cool milk in the world. Still living on her family's property, one of my best friends growing up, Avis Laws Collins, recanted to me the process: Grandma Mamie milked the cows twice daily, storing the milk in half-gallon jars for drinking. In a separate jar, fresh milk was allowed to sit for a while to become almost sour; we called it "clavour milk." That clavour milk, very similar to buttermilk today, would sit for a while, as long as two weeks. The beauty of this magnificent process is that the CREAM from the milk always rises to the top. Once the cream rose to the top, it was scooped off and put in a separate container. Then she would take the cream and a few pinches of salt and put it in the churn. The old-fashioned churn is similar to an ice cream maker today. After hand churning for an hour or two, the mixture thickened. Avis's job was to hand crank the churner until it became thick, producing butter. The thickened end product was poured into a pound and a half ceramic bowl, eventually softening itself up.

Let's discover how this process relates to your personal and business life. Once you are successful and rise to the top of your field, pay it forward by reaching out, lending a hand to someone else who is still grazing in the pasture. Your churning hand produces more sweet cream and butter. More cream and butter produces better families, peaceful communities, thriving businesses, viable states, and prospering nations. The fascinating lesson from churning and making butter is ingenious and can be applied to every arena of your personal, professional, and spiritual life. YOU represent the perfected production. Of course, life will have you grazing the field seeking for nourishing food, with some days feeling like you need to stay in the pasture and not seek any water. The economy may make you feel like you're being churned in that machine, going around and around in circles. The joy comes when YOU, the cream, rise to the top. Only your mental state, your attitudes, or desires allow you to stay at the bottom—you will eventually rise to the top. We were not promised great days every day of our lives; yet we were promised joy in the morning, if we continued to press our way through.

When standing up for your values, stay consistent and persistent without waffling and wallowing; the sweet cream does rise to the top. It really doesn't matter if it takes longer for your butter to be churned; most important is that you get to the top. You may even have setbacks during which you feel like you're the cow, grazing back in the fields for the right food and nourishment to survive. Stay focused and keep your eye on the prize. If you believe it, you can achieve it.

The final lesson here is that if you give more than you get paid for; your reward is continued profitability. We're all in sales and when you provide your family, your clients, your community, and those you serve more than they ask for or pay for, you keep them coming back. You see, Granny made pound cakes with Grandma Mamie's homemade butter. Usually weekly, she'd send us up the road to get her a pound of butter. I never realized until talking with Avis that it was actually a pound and a half. Grandma Mamie was an entrepreneur who knew more about profitability than many CEOs today. She was more interested in building lasting relationships than a few transactions, as people would come from all over the county, far and near to buy butter. She'd occasionally just give it to you. Now this is a life-fulfilling prophetic act and lesson.

A Century Captured

Granny's mustard seed faith has brought her to a land of abundance. This abundance is not measured in wealth or material possessions but a legacy filled with seeds of love, passion, compassion, and service. A living testimony as described in James 2:5: "God chose the poor of this world to be rich in faith and heirs of the kingdom which he promised to those who love Him." In 1910, although she was lacking in material possessions, she was filled with the richness of faith, the size of a mere grain. When one has unlimited material resources, it sometimes hinders faith, and they place their hopes, dreams, and security in their wealth instead of God. When life gets out of control, twirling us like a tsunami, we have no choice but to lean on our faith. As a nation, our vulnerabilities have us primed to exercise our faith. This mustard seed faith coupled with "trust in the Lord with all your heart and lean not on your own understanding (Proverbs 3:5)," means abundance will be rediscovered.

Granny has a strong will and backbone, inherited from her parents, particularly Granddaddy Wiley. Grandaddy was a tall and stately man. His physique, poise, and wisdom seemed to tower over trees. Sketched in my mind are porch moments with him just talking about life. He had apparently mellowed by the time I was a teenager and began living with him. I was the last grandchild to live with Granddaddy and to share these moments. In our family, the oldest grandchild (great-grandchild in my case) went to stay with Granddaddy, performing household chores, cooking, and cleaning. Prior to driving my school bus route, my duty was to cook a piping hot breakfast before cranking up the bus at 6:00 am. We're talking a real breakfast, not toast and juice. Granddaddy's favorite was homemade biscuits, grits, eggs, and liver pudding. I am *A Chosen Seed*, as I got to share these special moments before he died two months prior to my high school graduation. He knew that he had helped to equip this SEED with all of the ingredients for success with our porch moments as my fondest memories. Ironically, this book was written during great porch moments reflecting peacefully with the birds, squirrels, and deer roaming.

Now a "Grandy" to two beautiful grandchildren, Deanna Kaylene and Donovan William Bennett, over the years I have coined a few-century inspired *Grannyisms*™ of my own. These flourishing seeds filled with abundance will provide a lamp to your personal lives and light in the corporate world.

❧ Hire your weaknesses, but hire integrity over skill.

This makes the team stronger, adding skill sets that compliment the current team dynamics. In hiring your weaknesses, always, always hire integrity over skill. Remember we said earlier that experience comes from bad judgment and experience is the best teacher? Those may be true statements but it's a hefty price to pay. Never lessen the lesson! My experience has shown that the highest skilled low-integrity performer will always cost you in more long-lasting ways, more significant than dollars and cents. If a lower skilled, yet high-integrity individual makes an error, you may have to waive fees, provide complimentary services, or earn less profitability for a sale, but you've only lost dollars and cents. When a higher skilled, low-integrity performer makes an error, the error is often deliberate, self-serving, and with deceitful tactics. This performer jeopardizes your corporate reputation, the legacy and traditions on which your foundation rests, significant licensing and bonding requirements, and your professional dignity. The latter example will cost you things that money cannot buy: your priceless and extraordinary values. When hiring, *A Chosen Seed* chooses excellence and integrity over skill.

⚘ Selflessness will always prevail.

Selflessness will always prevail, not selfishness. Though she had limited means, I saw Granny give and give to others, which modeled unconditional love and a selfless spirit. As a matter of fact, there were times when she knew she had been wronged but was the first person on the wrong-doer's doorsteps with a basket filled with piping hot biscuits, fresh vegetables, well-seasoned chicken pastry and rice along with a sweet potato pie or cobbler when they became ill. This is true selflessness and servant-hood. Her model was to turn the other cheek. With this model, I have always been a giver to a fault as well, which is why I've never understood people who had selfish motives. Selfish people work twice as hard to get to the starting gate, spending all their time trying to figure out how they can obtain more for less or receive without paying the price. Selfish people have created the game of shortcuts and possess an earned graduate degree with summa cum laude honors. The graduate and honors degree provide benefits and rewards for a period of time (in some cases it seems like a lifetime) only to end up behind the eight ball, with a seemingly collapsed roof over their body. While they know that selfishness isn't healthy, some people just have to learn the hard way. What a costly tuition only to have a worthless degree. Selfish individuals compete with others needlessly, depriving them of joy and the rewards of cooperation, teamwork, strategically solving problems, and consensus building. Selflessness will always prevail over selfishness.

⚘ **A selfish spirit spins like a pinwheel.**

People who have selfish spirits never stop spinning. They continuously spin their wheels, always trying to make sure they succeed, even at the expense of others. They mask it by being overly engaged or happy about others, while only seeking to devour their victims. Life, in their minds, is all about them, spinning like a pinwheel. When a pinwheel spins, the force of the wind keeps it spinning around and around, and the various colors looking beautiful. The problem with a pinwheel is that when the wind stops, the pinwheel stops. A selfish-spirited individual is always looking for a force of wind to keep spinning until their true colors are finally revealed. Be careful with those pinwheels in your life; they are proficient spinners, living a life of emptiness, always grasping for the wind.

⚡ **Don't go into battle with unhappy soldiers; they'll get you killed.**

Our family, friends, business, human capital, and valued relationships are our most prized possessions. It's important that they are happy and productive, which increases efficiency, motivation, and survival skills. We all have days when we're not at our best but those days should be few and far between. Unhappy people are downers and will spread havoc, discord, and a contentious atmospheric pressure that will camouflage Granny's lye soap as a sweet perfumed solution. If your household or team has genuine, habitual, everyday unhappy people, you need to arm yourself with a breastplate of selective words and armor. The power of unhappy soldiers will destroy a nation or business. *A Chosen Seed* removes these soldiers from battle in order to preserve the morale of the entire unit, protecting the legacy.

⚡ **Inspect what you expect.**

This is a saying that I coined as business banking sales manager for a major bank over a decade ago. Business and commercial bankers at this financial institution were not accustomed to a strong sales culture of goals, strict performance reviews, and accountability. As a sales leader in your home or at work, if you don't inspect what you expect, the expectations are meaningless and give room to low-expectation performers. Performers who "far exceed expectations" are in a minority. In these tougher sales and economic times, the weak are easily exposed and the "cream always rises to the top."

꒐ **Feedback is an extraordinary mustard seed gift.**

If someone unwraps it for you, treasure it. Constructive feedback corrects habits and behaviors. Can you imagine who you'd be or what your life would be like if your parents never corrected or disciplined you? We'd all be a mess. If someone gives you constructive feedback, instead of receiving it negatively, take it as a love offering, sowing seeds of greatness into your life. Feedback seeds are extraordinary, as powerful as a mustard seed. If you allow the seed to grow, watch your transformation blossom into a sprawling beautiful thirty-foot tree.

꒐ **Your child is a mirror, a sharp reflection of reality.**

When you look in a mirror, you see a reflective view of yourself with the beauty as well as your flaws. A mirror focuses light, distorts reflective images, and can also show a reversed image. Because of their innocence and honesty, a child has a special way of painting the picture of reality and weaknesses that one has no desire to admit. The sharp reflection of a child's mirror is as powerful as any sword.

꒐ **Greed won't prosper.**

Greed is like a bottomless pit. Whether corporate or personal, it won't prosper. It reminds me of Edgar Allan Poe's short story "The Pit and the Pendulum." Whether you choose to jump into the pit or get sliced in half by the pendulum—the inevitable outcome is the same. Decisions have consequences. The consequence is death. Whether you choose greed in your business practices or the love of money, it has the same outcome. We all need money to survive; it's how we treat people as we obtain it. And by the way, the Good Book does not say that "money is the root of all evil." 1 Timothy 6:10a actually says, "The _love_ of money is the root of all evil."(KJV) The love of money produces greed, and that greed will never prosper.

- **Quality shocks—everybody doesn't expect it.**

Quality shocks and roars like a lion when you exceed expectations. While you may have certain expectations for yourself, your children, and those within your influence, anticipate the expectations that others have set for you to be at an uneven bar. When quality exceeds people's expectations, it not only shocks but leaves them bewildered, even dumbfounded. You see, there are individuals, even business leaders and managers, who have low expectations because of their perceived differences of others despite their qualifications. When this happens (and it will, just keep on living), smile and continue to shine. From my personal and corporate experience, never diminish quality or lower your standards to pad the low expectations of others and make them feel comfortable. It is absolutely permissible to pursue and have a strong passion for excellence. Because quality shocks, that's their problem. Never allow it to be yours or succumb to their level. I shared with a banking executive at one time, "How dare you set a bar for me? No one—and I mean no one—sets any limits for me, except me." Even though quality continues to shock others, always Pursue Excellence!

- **Don't take for granted what you see on the outside.**

Whether it's your size, ethnicity, gender, or perhaps a mental or physical challenge, you may get taken for granted merely by the outside persona. If this is one of your company's best practices (usually imbedded for years but unspoken), be aware that you are compromising the growth, stability, and revenue potential of all divisions. When you judge and take for granted someone merely by what you perceive from their outward appearances, your insecurities outshine everything. Try to mask it with all of the strong will that you have, but the real you overpowers and comes to light. Celebrate the differences of others because we are more alike than we are different. At first glance, taking one for granted may not seem like a big deal but over time, it's the same as carbon monoxide, an odorless gas—a silent killer.

⚶ Free is too expensive.

This is actually a saying that I coined and used with a potential client. There are times in developing and marketing yourself or your business that you have to provide more than you get paid for. That's how relationships are developed and nurtured. There is also a boiling point of being used and taken advantage of. When someone begins the dialogue with a desire to waive, decrease, or cleverly manipulate your fee structure, then they just want something for nothing. "Free is too expensive" means that your skill, expertise, and years of experience and knowledge are valuable and when you continue to give it all away, you devalue yourself. People don't take your power away from you; you give it to them. Furthermore, when you religiously provide free services, people don't value and appreciate it.

⚶ All poverty is not financial.

When we think of poverty, most of us immediately think of being poor when it comes to money. To be impoverished is to have a deficiency or a lack of anything. This can be a lack of skill, experience, intelligence, education, or even integrity. There are people or businesses that have strong financial means but have impoverished minds. The mindset and the culture under which we operate could be a ticking bomb, ready to blow up at any time. An impoverished mind is more detrimental than a lack of financial resources. The United Negro College Fund's branding speaks volumes: "a mind is a terrible thing to waste." A business culture is also a terrible thing to waste.

❧ Life's rainbow is full of P²LUGS and JOY

When traveling from Tyson's Corner near Washington, DC, for our family reunion this summer, a beautiful rainbow appeared in the sky. I was not only marveling at its beauty but the beauty of our strong family ties. We aren't perfect by any means, but there are wealth-building moments, legacies, and traditions that have been passed down for generations that will strengthen the many branches of the family tree to continue great works. Just as a rainbow is an arc of spectacular colors caused by a refraction of the sun's rays of rain, the band of parallel stripes blended at the rims is symmetrical to our family. Having watched Granny's centurion life and how she's interacted with family, friends, church, and community, the lessons can be impeccably applied to individuals and businesses alike as they have a strong symmetrical power for abundance.

Like a rainbow, your personal and professional life is full of p²lugs and joy. When you plug a lamp into an electrical socket, you expect to immediately receive light, visible enough to bring you out of darkness. Not necessarily so.

Some plugs have shortages and you may have to find alternative measures—another socket. Just because one electrical outlet isn't working, you don't stop until you find one that will bring you out of darkness. Your survival depends on these sources of light. These sources are:

❧   Prayer

Since these strategies are geared to elevating your business life as well as your personal endeavors, I can already hear someone saying, "I'd be fired if I took prayer to the workplace." While you may be absolutely correct, know that fervent prayer begins in your secret closet. A strong prayer life can effect change without you uttering a word in your corporate corridors. More importantly, it's the life you exhibit as you interact daily that has the most powerful effect on transformation. Remember, your life may be the only Bible that many people will ever read.

❧   Peace

Peace and harmony can cure many ills, adding a downpour of rain to diminish a raging fire. When working on team leadership for a desired goal particularly, peace and harmony travel the speed of an airplane exceeding its on-time arrival expectations. Peace and harmony provide a safe atmosphere for participants to work diligently to increased revenue efficiencies.

❧   Love: unconditional love.

Growing up, people didn't say, "I love you" verbally often, but there was absolutely no question that you were loved. Love was unconditional, believing and knowing it by people's actions, not just a verbalization. When a delicious meal was put on the table for your nourishment and enjoyment, that was love. When everyone in the community was concerned about your well-being and your success, that was love. When EVERY adult, not just your family but all of the Mamas in the community, took the time to impart wisdom to you, showing genuine compassion, that was love. Today, people say, "I love you" all the time, so much so in many cases, I wonder if the meaning has lost some of its luster. Now don't get me wrong, I will admit, particularly for women, we admonish, seek, and cherish affection and adore being told, "I love you" but there needs to be some action behind those words. Showing love when it's inconvenient is unconditional.

୬   Gratefulness

There's nothing better than having a grateful heart. We always told our young men when they were growing up, "People don't have to be nice to you. Always say thank you and write thank-you notes when people do something to enhance your life." A sincere and grateful heart will bring you a life of abundance through blessings of which your mind can't even conceive. Don't take for granted the small, everyday blessings. I was reminded of this at a visit at the Cancer Center of North Carolina. I was in the presence of people whose emotions ranged from finding out for the first time that they had cancer, to people in their last days on this earth battling Stage 4 cancer. The day that I was able to walk into the cancer center without my heavy boot on my right foot and leg, with no crutches and very little pain, other patients reacted with unconditional love, praises, gratefulness, and joy, relishing in *my* moment of recovery. With tears in his eyes a gentleman said, "Congratulations! Soon you will get to fire your hematologist. Not many of the people who come here get the opportunity to do that. You are blessed." Like a knife piercing through my heart, it replaced the little pain that I felt. The severe piercing was as potent as a pitchfork pulling the veins out of my leg just a few months earlier. At that moment, like a mustard seed, the miraculous progression from being pushed in a wheelchair with a full cast, to pushing a walker myself, to using a set of crutches with a full boot, to using one crutch and a boot, to walking solo in New Balance tennis shoes was astounding and forever pressed into my heart. The nurses and lab technicians rejoiced, as during my first visit it took four of them and an hour to get a few tubes of blood—blood so thick it was clotting in the tubes. God's omnipotent power was ever-present, like a brick being thrown to knock me in the head, reminding me that by HIS grace and mercy, I am indeed *A CHOSEN SEED* receiving the priceless gift of another chance to fulfill an abundant life.

❧ Joy

Joy is a cousin to gratefulness and the art of showing gratitude. I had witnessed my light and many candles lighting another. All the light in the world is meaningless without joy. Life's rainbow is definitely filled with prayer, peace, love—unconditionally—gratefulness, and joy. The full symmetrical imagery was prevalent with all of its colorful beauty.

⚶ **Know that you are *A CHOSEN Seed: from mustard seed to abundance*.**

Each of us are *Chosen* Seeds, bringing to fruition the visions in our lives. I'm sure Granny never gave much thought to what it fully means to be *A Chosen Seed*, for it is a part of her being. She didn't care about the real depth and breadth of being chosen; it was a way of life. She has lived for one hundred years not really having this comprehension and is modeled beautifully by the fruit of her seeds, each of us knowing that we are *A Chosen Seed* and shining examples for the world to emulate. Like Granny, knowing that we are *CHOSEN* Seeds, we are destined to produce:

- Abundance from amazing humility
- Bountiful fruit from small but strong foundational planting
- Opportunities from obedience
- Testimony from our tests
- Triumphs over our trials
- Glory from the guilt and shame
- Deliverance from downtrodden days
- Life fulfillment from loving unconditionally
- A renewed spirit from the ruts of life
- Hope from hopelessness
- Powerful ministry from our misery
- Destiny from despair
- Prosperity from pruning
- Peace from paying it forward
- Joy from our jacked-up situations
- Health and healing from our hurts

- Guiding light from the gutter
- Light for future legacies
- Satisfaction from servant-hood
- Wisdom from our wilderness experiences
- Victory from the true vine

A virtuous woman is a woman of strength, "her worth far above rubies." (Proverbs 31:10b) Granny provided and cared for her family unselfishly. When money was tight, she carried and covered them with prayer. At the centennial celebration, my cousin Brenda Hill cited this befitting scripture from Proverbs 31:25-31 describing this *Chosen Seed* and virtuous woman:

> Strength and honor are her clothing
> She shall rejoice in time to come
> She opens her mouth with wisdom
> And on her tongue is the law of kindness
> She watches over the ways of her household
> And does not eat the bread of idleness
> Her children rise up and call her blessed
> Her husband also, and he praises her
> Many daughters have done well
> But you excel them all.
> Charm is deceitful and beauty is passing
> But a woman who fears the LORD, she shall be praised
> Give her the fruit of her hands
> And let her own works praise her in the gates.

In capturing this century of life, a song by Luther Barnes and The Sunset Jubilaires titled, "It's A Mighty Good Thing to be Chosen" sums it up:

It's a mighty good thing, to be chosen by God
It's a mighty good thing, to be chosen to serve
So don't ever complain, when HE calls your name
The job might seem hard, but you'll get a special reward
When you're chosen by God.

Some people think that they're being picked on
When they're asked to do something good
They make excuses and say I'm not able
But all the while they really could
But don't hold back and don't be afraid
Just go on and do the best you can
My God will be right there to work it all out for you
Just make one step and He'll see you through.

God called Moses on a mountain top
He told him to lead his people out of Egypt land
But Moses complained and said, Lord I don't have the
speech
Surely you must have the wrong man
But you see God knew his weakness, He also knew his
strengths
Yes, he already knew what Moses could do—
Just look what he did
Moses took up his staff and went on down to Egypt land
And he led the people out with a mighty hand.

Well, I heard somebody say
That if you don't use your gift, you'll lose your gift
In other words you are to be glad
If you are blessed enough to have a gift
And to be chosen to do a work for the Lord

Because that means that you're special in the eyesight of God.

It's a mighty good thing, to be chosen by God
It's a mighty good thing, to be chosen to serve
So don't ever complain, when HE calls your name
The job might seem hard, but you'll get a special reward
When you're *CHOSEN* by God.

Know that you are chosen out of the world (John 15:19) and appointed that you should go and bear fruit (John 15:16) not just for yourself but to better your family, community and business – spreading hope, love, peace and economic prosperity throughout the world. Being *CHOSEN* has great rewards and great responsibilities, "For many are called, but few are chosen." (Matthew 22:14)

Hard work combined with faith of a mustard seed will bring all of your visions masterfully to fruition. "God chose the poor of this world to be rich in faith and heirs of the kingdom which he promised to those who love him." (James 2:5) You too are an heir to true abundance!

Know that you are A CHOSEN Seed: from mustard seed to abundance!

Grannyisms™ by Chapter

CHAPTER 1

Soil Preparation

Foundation

- When you have faith of a mustard seed, you can do anything but fail.

- Make sure you have a strong foundation.

- Hard work will take you to a land flowing with milk and honey.

- Life is simpler when you plow around the stumps.

- The early bird gets the worm.

- If you believe your vaccine will work, then inject it in your own veins.

- A slack hand makes you poor.

- Live your life so folks can trust you.

- Everything that glitters ain't gold.

- Your word is your bond.

- Winners do what losers don't want to.

- You will reap what you sow

- What goes around comes around.

- You can't make a horse out of a mule.

- Be careful what you hitch your wagon up to.

- Before you try to pull someone out of the water, make sure your feet are on solid ground.

- When life gives you lemons, make lemonade.

- You never get a second chance to make a first impression.

- You can't live but one day at a time.

- A small hole can sink a large ship.

- Hatred is like acid.

- You can't get freshwater and saltwater from the same hole.

- If you don't have a seat at the table, you'll be part of the menu.

- We are the source of our own problems.

- A man's venom poisons himself more than others.

- You don't know what's in my alabaster box.

- Rash words thrust like a sword.

- If the cake is bad, you don't need the frosting.

- Keep oil in your lamp.

- Waste not, want not.

- We make our habits, and then our habits break us.

- There's no testimony without a test.

- Don't let Him catch you with your work undone.

- A penny saved is a penny earned.

- Every penny has a purpose.

- If you never save any money, you'll never have any.

- Always save for a rainy day.

- An idle mind is a devil's workshop.

- Parents who want to train their children in the way they should go, must first go in the way they want their children to go.

- It doesn't matter what's on the table but what's sitting in the chairs.

- Every tub has to stand on its own bottom.

- Every chair has to stand on its own legs.

- A chain is only as strong as its weakest link.

- You are always on stage.

- A house divided can't stand.

- Be wary of fair-weather friends.

- Don't waste your time learning the tricks of the trade; learn the trade.

- The one who wins is the one who thinks he can.

- Don't get too big for your britches.

- Stay in your lane.

- If you sweep around your own front door; you won't have time to sweep around mine.

- I'm not driving that bus.

- There's more than one way to skin a cat.

- Be careful what you ask for; you just might get it.

- Don't bite off more than you can chew.

- You can't have your cake and eat it too.

- What's good for the goose is good for the gander.

- Do it right the first time. It'll take you twice as long to do it over.

- Build your hopes on things eternal.

- Ninety-nine and a half won't do.

CHAPTER 2

Planting Seeds

The Vision

- Ain't no harvest without seed time.

- Seeds bear fruit.

- Bloom where you are planted.

- Decisions have lifelong consequences.

- If you're not careful, you might end up in the hole you're digging for somebody else.

- Common sense ain't common to everybody.

- In our good days, our weaknesses are revealed. In our bad days, our strengths are revealed.

- Don't burn bridges. You just might have to cross back over them.

- Actions speak louder than words.

- Talk is cheap.

- Empty wagons make a whole lot of noise.

- You can't take back what's already out of your mouth.

- It's not what you say but how you say it.

- If you harvest thorns, look at your own garden.

- The grass is not always greener on the other side.

- If you think the grass is greener on the other side, go ahead and buy you a new lawn mower.

- To belittle is to be little.

- You never know what's going on behind closed doors.

- A dog that carries a bone will bring one.

- Let sleeping dogs lie.

- A bird in the hand is worth two in the bush.

- You're jumping out the frying pan into the fire.

- He who carries the cross carries the burden.

- That's not your cross to bear.

- If you can't say nothing good about somebody, then don't say nothing at all.

- Foxes have holes.

- A hint to the wise is sufficient.

- When you know who you are, you don't have to waste time trying to be somebody else.

- We are all manufacturers: making goods, making trouble, or making excuses.

- Excuses are nothing but justified lies.

- Making excuses don't change the truth.

- If it sounds too good to be true, it probably is.

- If you don't stand for something, you'll fall for anything.

- You can't straddle the fence.

- If you sit around waiting for your ship to come in, you might miss the boat.

- Nothing beats a failure but a try.

- Hard work ain't never killed nobody.

- The grave is full of great ideas.

- Don't try to keep up with the Joneses.

- Live beneath your means.

- By the time you can make ends meet, the ends might move.

- You have to have two things to make a good marriage. You gotta to find the right person and you gotta BE the right person.

- When trouble comes your way, you must be doing something right.

- No problems, no progress.

CHAPTER 3

Watering

Nourishment

- ❧ **You don't miss your water until the well runs dry.**

- ❧ **Your mouth is full of deep waters.**

- ❧ **You can't appreciate the sunshine until you've had some rain.**

- ❧ **Don't rain on other folks' parade.**

- ❧ **All the dirt will come out in the wash.**

- ❧ **Don't throw the baby out with the bathwater.**

- ❧ **Blood is thicker than water.**

- ❧ **A little fire can kindle a big forest.**

- ❧ **A burning fire is better than a flame not yet lit.**

- ❧ **You can't see the forest for the trees.**

- ❧ **Worry is a mental tornado.**

- ❧ **Don't worry about tomorrow. Today has enough trouble of its own.**

- Worry is like a dog chasing its own tail.

- An ounce of prevention is worth a pound of cure.

- People that don't ever do more than they get paid for, never get paid for more than what they do.

- People who are easy to please are hard to satisfy.

- Do all things without murmuring and complaining.

- It's easy to spend someone else's money.

- How can you look at the speck in someone else's eye when you have a plank in yours?

- A hard head makes a soft behind.

- If the shoe fits, wear it.

- Two can keep a secret if one of them is dead.

- Nobody knows your business unless you tell them.

- Silence is golden.

- Silence is healing for all ailments.

- The less said, the better.

- Hold your piece and let the Lord fight your battle.

- Just because snow is on the chimney does not mean there's no fire in the stove.

- Every closed eye ain't sleep.

- Every open eye can't see.

- Be careful how you live. Somebody's always watching.

- Everybody you meet knows something you don't. Learn from them.

- The blind are leading the blind.

- You can't pour piss out of a boot, even if it's turned upside down.

- You ain't got a pot to piss in nor a window to throw it out of.

- You are like a fish out of water.

- Don't rock the boat.

- You can lead a horse to the water but you can't make him drink it.

- Don't ever let your left hand know what your right hand is doing.

- That's a crying shame.

- That's calling the kettle black.

⯈ **You can either sink or swim.**

⯈ **Faith without works is dead.**

⯈ **A boat in a harbor is safe, but in time the bottom will rot out.**

⯈ **Be the captain of your own ship.**

CHAPTER 4

Nurturing

Nurture

- ⚥ **Look for the good in the bad.**

- ⚥ **Charity begins at home.**

- ⚥ **We are all a work in progress.**

- ⚥ **Great timber grows on both trees and man.**

- ⚥ **The stronger the wind, the stronger the tree.**

- ⚥ **Please and thank you never go out of style.**

- ⚥ **Don't look a gift horse in the mouth.**

- ⚥ **Don't judge a book by its cover.**

- ⚥ **Don't spread yourself too thin.**

- ⚥ **You can't burn the candle at both ends.**

- ⚥ **You can win the battle but lose the war.**

- ⚥ **Spare the rod, spoil the child.**

- ❧ Parents who want to train up their children in the way they should go, must first go in the way they want their children to go.

- ❧ Life and death are in the power of the tongue.

- ❧ A quarrel starts out like a tiny hole with a trickle of water. If it ain't stopped, the trickle can become a flood.

- ❧ Kind words turn away a fuss; harsh ones stir it up.

- ❧ You can't slide uphill.

- ❧ You've got just enough rope to hang yourself.

- ❧ Don't go to bed mad with each other.

- ❧ If you don't use your talents, you'll lose them.

- ❧ Something in the milk ain't clean.

- ❧ I might have been born at night but not last night.

- ❧ When one door closes, another opens.

- ❧ A quitter never wins; a winner never quits.

- ❧ Winners do what losers don't want to.

CHAPTER 5

Fruitfulness

Enjoying the Beauty

- ❧ **You can tell a tree by the fruit it bears.**

- ❧ **A fig tree don't bear olives.**

- ❧ **Don't run after what's for you. If you live right, it'll run after you.**

- ❧ **Don't chase after your blessings.**

- ❧ **Your reputation will travel more miles than you ever will.**

- ❧ **Your reputation precedes you.**

- ❧ **Be the salt that you are.**

- ❧ **Keep doing good things for people and don't worry about if they ever find out.**

- ❧ **Nobody hides a lit lamp under their bed.**

- ❧ **Don't stay where you ain't welcome.**

- ❧ **Go where you are celebrated, not tolerated.**

- ❦ Honor your mother and father.

- ❦ You ain't fully dressed until you put on a smile.

- ❦ Give me my flowers while I'm living.

- ❦ Slow down and smell the roses.

- ❦ When in doubt, do the right thing.

- ❦ Many people can see...but only a few know what they are looking for.

- ❦ Knowledge is worth more than gold.

- ❦ Close your mouth and open your ears. Opportunity knocks softly.

- ❦ Let go of the past.

- ❦ You can't cry over spilled milk.

- ❦ Beauty is but skin deep.

- ❦ There are no degrees of honesty.

- ❦ Fast money flies fast.

- ❦ Easy come, easy go.

- ❦ You're writing your tombstone each day.

- ❦ Leave everything a little bit better than you found it.

- Live life like an exclamation, not an explanation.

- Don't let other folks steal your joy.

- What you weave in time, you'll wear in eternity.

- More pain, more gain.

- More gain, more pain.

- The easy way is not always the best way.

- The apple didn't fall far from the tree.

- Who yo (your) people?

- May the works I've done speak for me. May the life I live speak for me.

- It's not what you know but who you know.

- It's not who you know but who knows you.

- Even a cracked pot can be used.

CHAPTER 6

Pruning

Being Pruned

- ᛣ **Everything that bears fruit gotta be pruned.**

- ᛣ **Get rid of stuff that ain't bearing no fruit.**

- ᛣ **God don't like ugly.**

- ᛣ **Don't ever lessen the lesson.**

- ᛣ **Some people enjoy staying in hell 'cause they know the names of all the streets.**

- ᛣ **People in hell want ice water.**

- ᛣ **If you lay down with dogs, you'll get fleas.**

- ᛣ **Iron sharpens iron.**

- ᛣ **Practice what you preach.**

- ᛣ **If you make your bed hard, you'll have to lay in it.**

- ᛣ **Don't expect people to listen to your advice and ignore your example.**

- Troubles don't last always.

- Play with fire and see don't you get burned.

- You can't walk on coals and not get your feet burnt.

- Weeping may endure for a night but joy comes in the morning.

- What's done in the dark will eventually come to light.

- A leech only knows two things: Gimme and Gimme mo (Give me and Give me more)

- Pigs get fatter while hogs get slaughtered.

- Don't bore people with all your problems. They have enough of their own.

- Don't judge anybody until you've walked a mile in their shoes.

- If you don't like something in somebody, change it in yourself.

- Experience is the best teacher.

- If you ain't never had hard times, just keep on living.

- Ponder the path of your feet.

- It's time for you to be eating solid foods.

- Anything that's dead need to be buried.

- If a robin can say thank you, you can do it too.

- If you can't stand the heat, get out of the kitchen.

- God won't put no more on you than you can bear.

- There's always a blue sky behind the darkest cloud.

- Why do you keep knocking your head against the brick wall?

- The truth hurts.

- Your enemies will tell you your faults.

- Let's put all the liars in the same room at the same time.

- There are two sides to every story.

- There are three sides to every story: his, hers, and the truth.

- Just like churning makes butter, harsh words make fire.

- Watch how you treat folks climbing up the ladder—they may have to catch you on the way down.

- Be careful how you treat people because you never know who's going to give you your last drink of water.

- Be careful how you treat people; you don't know whose behind you might have to kiss before you leave this world.

- You can't get to tomorrow by holding on to yesterday.

- Don't ever say what your children won't do. They will make you eat your words.

- Everything in moderation.

- There's some good in everybody.

- You're putting the cart before the horse.

- I'm on the other side of through.

- Letting the cat out of the bag is a whole lot easier than putting it back in.

- The man with no shoes felt sorry for himself until he met a man with no feet.

- When you find yourself in a hole, stop digging.

- The biggest troublemaker in your life is staring you in the mirror.

- Wallow with pigs and you'll surely get dirty.

- Two wrongs don't make a right.

- This too shall pass.

CHAPTER 7

Abundance

Abundant Living

- The Lord is my shepherd, I shall not want.

- Be careful how you live. You might be the only BIBLE a lot of people read.

- Lord (pronounced LAWD by Granny) remember me.

- Count it all joy.

- God loves a cheerful giver.

- Stay prayed up.

- The Lord takes care of babies and fools.

- All things work together for good.

- I can do all things through Christ who strengthens me.

- Seven days without God makes you weak.

- The Lord will make a way somehow.

- He'll make a way out of no way.

- Words like deeds bear fruit.

- Riches ain't measured by money.

- Be the salt that you are.

- Tasteless salt is worthless.

- Let your little light shine.

- The best thing you'll ever have is your reputation.

- A candle don't lose nothing by lighting another one.

- If you want your dreams to come true, then wake up.

- All things are possible if you only believe.

- Figure out early if the glass is half full or half empty.

- It's better to limp all the way to heaven than not to get there at all.

- Give credit where credit is due.

- Good judgment comes from experience. Experience comes from bad judgment.

- Don't put all your eggs in one basket.

- Keep several irons in the fire.

- Different strokes for different folks.

- Count your blessings; name them one by one.

- When praises go up, blessings come down.

- Praise Him from whom all blessings flow.

- A good name is worth more than silver and gold.

- To whom much is given, much is expected.

- Hard work beats talent when talent don't beat hard work.

- When you forgive your enemies, it messes up their head.

- Ain't nothing new under the sun.

- A penny wise and a pound foolish.

- God works in mysterious ways.

- He didn't bring me this far to leave me.

- Do what you can live with!

- Don't be so heavenly bound that you're no earthly good.

- Your setback is gonna wind up being a miracle.

- I don't know what the future holds, but I know who holds the future.

- Cherish your front row.

- Cream always rises to the top.

CONCLUSION

A Century Captured

• • •

- ❧ Hire your weaknesses, but hire integrity over skill.

- ❧ Selflessness will always prevail.

- ❧ A selfish spirit spins like a pinwheel.

- ❧ Don't go into battle with unhappy soldiers; they'll get you killed.

- ❧ Inspect what you expect.

- ❧ Feedback is an extraordinary mustard seed gift.

- ❧ Your child is a mirror, a sharp reflection of reality.

- ❧ Greed won't prosper.

- ❧ Quality shocks—everybody doesn't expect it.

- ❧ **Don't take for granted what you see on the outside.**

- ❧ **Free is too expensive.**

- ❧ **All poverty is not financial.**

- ❧ **Life's rainbow is full of P²LUGS and JOY.**

- ❧ **Know that you are *A CHOSEN Seed: from mustard seed to abundance.***

You can't celebrate a
16 x 20 idea with
a 3 x 5 mind.

Made in the
USA
Columbia, SC

80090364R00133